STUDY GUIDE

FOR

COME INTO MY TRADING ROOM

BOOKS BY DR. ALEXANDER ELDER

Trading for a Living

Study Guide for Trading for a Living

Rubles to Dollars:
  Making Money on Russia's Exploding Financial Frontier

STUDY GUIDE
FOR
COME INTO MY TRADING ROOM

Dr. Alexander Elder
www.elder.com

John Wiley & Sons, Inc.
New York • Chichester • Weinheim • Brisbane • Singapore • Toronto

Published by John Wiley & Sons, Inc.
Published simultaneously in Canada.

This publication is designed to provide accurate and authoritative information in regard
to the subject matter covered. It is sold with the understanding that the publisher is not
engaged in rendering professional services. If professional advice or other expert assis-
tance is required, the services of a competent professional person should be sought.

ISBN 0-471-22540-1

Printed in the United States of America.

10 9 8 7 6 5 4 3 2 1

CONTENTS

STUDY GUIDE FOR COME INTO MY TRADING ROOM

Think of the millions of people who throw money at stocks, options, and futures. Probably less than one percent of them ever pick up a trading book. Only a tiny fraction of those perform any learning exercises or take tests. If you can work through this *Study Guide*, grade your performance, then study and retake some of the tests if necessary, you will belong to a small sophisticated minority.

It is easy to sit at a lecture, sagely nod your head, and think you understand everything. What if someone asks you a question about that lecture a week or a month later? Will you be able to answer, or will you have forgotten by then?

It took me three years to write *Come into My Trading Room*, yet a person can read it in just a few days. Do you expect to get full value out of it after a quick read? Or will you return, reread, review, and underline key sections and paragraphs? I created this *Study Guide* to help you grasp the main ideas in my book, expose blind spots, and achieve a deeper degree of understanding.

Do not rush yourself through this workbook. Take the tests one chapter at a time and keep returning to the original source until you get that chapter right. Then move to the next one. There is nothing wrong with taking several weeks to work through this book. Quality is more important than speed.

HOW THIS BOOK
IS ORGANIZED

The first section, Financial Trading for Babes in the Woods, quizzes you on the essential basics of trading. It asks about the efficient market theory, account size, and external barriers to winning, as well as market data and types of analysis. Rate your answers on the scales that are provided in each chapter. If you get a high grade, move on to the next chapter, but if your score is low, return to the main book and work through the basics before going any further.

Once you have covered the basics, it is time to move on to the three M's of successful trading, starting with the first—Mind. Questions in the second chapter deal with trading psychology, causes of losing, trading attitude, and, of course, discipline. Rate your answers on the scale. If your score is high, move on; otherwise, return to the main book. Many brilliant people fail in trading; no technical tools can help those whose minds are not in gear with the markets.

The second M—Method—is covered in several chapters. First, the chapter on basic charting quizzes you on classical technical analysis. The next chapter, on indicators, delves into moving averages, channels, MACD, Force Index, Elder-ray, and Stochastic. The next chapter, on trading, asks questions about system testing, timeframes, and Triple Screen. Feel free to skip the chapter on day-trading if you do not day-trade. Finally, there is a chapter that asks about new, revolutionary methods presented in the main book—the Impulse System and SafeZone stops.

Money management is the key skill that separates winners from losers. This chapter quizzes you about the 2% and the 6% Rules, mathematical expectation and position sizing. Make sure you answer each question right, and if not, return to the main book. Nothing less than a perfect score is acceptable in this chapter!

We conclude the *Study Guide* with a chapter called The Organized Trader. A person who is serious about his success has to organize his decision-making process and record-keeping. Questions in this chapter deal with trading records such as the equity curve, trading spreadsheet, and trader's diary. They cover time management, setting priorities, and rating your performance.

The charts in the *Study Guide* go beyond illustrating key analytic points. Each comes with questions about what you would do at the right edge. Signals tend to be clearly visible in the middle of the chart, but grow foggy as you get closer to the hard right edge. That's where you have to make trading decisions, in the atmosphere of uncertainty. This *Study Guide* is designed to train you to decide at that crucial barrier where people make or lose money.

Take your time as you go through the questions and exercises. Some questions may be hard, but hang on and work through them. A boot camp may feel overwhelming to a soldier, but it is designed to toughen him, so that he may survive the battle and come back alive and victorious.

QUESTIONS

FINANCIAL TRADING FOR BABES IN THE WOODS

Trading is serious business, no less so than building a house or teaching calculus. Being smart and having good ideas is not enough for winning. You must understand the mechanics of the markets and the essential principles of analysis and risk control.

You need to learn the key facts and rules before entering your first trade. The first chapter of the *Study Guide* tests your knowledge of some of those concepts. Answer these eight questions and write down your answers. Go to the Answers section, check your responses, and then enter your grade for each answer in the first column of the spreadsheet. There are five columns to enable you to return at a later date, retake the test, compare your results, and measure your progress.

Questions	Trial 1	Trial 2	Trial 3	Trial 4	Trial 5
1					
2					
3					
4					
5					
6					
7					
8					
Total points					

Question 1—Decision Making

Match the statements on the decision-making process with the type of trader.

1. A person hears a tip at a party and buys that stock in the morning.

2. A person hears a tip at a party and spends the next morning researching that stock and the industry group.

3. A person hears several people gossiping about a stock at a party and pulls it up on his computer with a view to selling it short.

4. A person sees a TV show about a famous investor and buys the stocks that he mentions.

5. A person reads a news release regarding disappointing earnings from a high-tech company and pulls up its chart the next day to see how it reacts to the report.

6. A person buys a stock after receiving a call from a relative working for a penny stock company who tells him of that firm's technological breakthrough that has not yet been disclosed to the public.

A. Investor

B. Trader

C. Gambler

Question 2—Efficient Market Theory

Which of the following statements regarding the efficient market theory are true and which are false?

1. All traders focus on maximizing profits and minimizing losses.

2. The outcome of any single trade is largely a matter of luck.

3. A trader whose account has increased after a year of active trading is very lucky.

4. Trading in a room with a group of people leads to more objective decisions.

5. Markets become more efficient when they become less volatile.

Question 3—Trading Choices

Match the following statements with the trading terms:

1. Finding these points is the hardest aspect of trading.

2. Buy when a rally accelerates, and sell when it starts losing speed.

3. These must be planned in advance; do not chase the markets.

4. This is the most often ignored aspect of trading.

5. Buy when a downside breakout starts pulling back up into the range, and liquidate within the range.

A. Countertrend trading

B. Entries

C. Money management

D. Momentum trading

E. Exits

Question 4—Stocks, Options, and Futures

Match the following statements with one or more of the trading vehicles.

1. The buyer must be right on the vehicle, price, and time.

2. This is a certificate of business ownership.

3. Money management skills are essential for success.

4. This is a contract for future delivery.

5. It's OK to buy cheap, but not OK to buy down.

A. Stocks

B. Futures

C. Options

Question 5—Barriers to Winning

Match each statement with one or more of the external barriers to winning.

1. They impact your account more than market trends.

2. They must be monitored so as not to exceed a small percentage of your account.

3. This is the distance between the price at which you place a market order and at which it is executed.

4. This is a meaningless percentage of your account.

5. This is an inevitable cost of entering markets.

A. Commissions

B. Slippage

C. Expenses

D. None

Question 6—Account Size

Five traders with similar levels of skill and all using stops enter the stock market. Which is likely to generate the highest percentage return?

1. $50,000 account; $5,000 maximum stop on any trade

2. $15,000 account; $1,500 maximum stop on any trade

3. $250,000 account; $50,000 maximum stop on any trade

4. $50,000 account; $1,000 maximum stop on any trade

5. $250,000 account; $5,000 maximum stop on any trade

Question 7—Market Data

Which of the following statements are true?

1. Real-time data is essential for timing entries and exits.

2. The more markets you follow, the more money you will make trading.

3. You must keep abreast of earnings reports for the stocks you follow.

4. Futures can sell for less than the cost of production.

5. Having 12 months' worth of daily charts makes weekly charts un-necessary.

6. Good software makes up for traders' inexperience.

A. 1 and 2

B. 2 and 3

C. 3 and 4

D. 4 and 5

E. 5 and 6

Question 8—Types of Analysis

Match each phrase with the types of analysis.

1. Studies economic supply and demand

2. Forecasts future prices

3. Studies crowd behavior

4. Can be fully automated

5. Serves as a basis of trading decisions

A. Fundamental analysis

B. Technical analysis

C. Both

D. Neither

MIND—
THE DISCIPLINED TRADER

Your personality is the key component of your trading success. Your thoughts, feelings, and attitudes have an immediate and direct impact on what happens to your account and whether it rises or falls. No level of computer power and no amount of technical expertise will do a trader any good if his mind is unsettled.

One day, if you get the chance, rent *Solaris*, a film by the late, great director Andrei Tarkovski. In this sci-fi film, a planet that has been bombarded by the scientists responds by reaching into their minds, extracting their most painful memories, and recreating those experiences for them. They must come to terms with those memories and resolve their old conflicts before becoming capable of getting in touch with the planet. Markets act like that planet in the sense that they reach deep into our minds, find our weaknesses, and hit us in our weak spots.

Greed, fear, carelessness, sloth, and other sins of omission or commission make successful trading difficult or impossible for most people. You have to look into the mirror, record your actions, recognize what you are doing wrong, and then correct your attitudes. Becoming a successful trader means becoming a more balanced and mature human being.

Questions	Trial 1	Trial 2	Trial 3	Trial 4	Trial 5
9					
10					
11					
12					
13					
14					
15					
16					
17					
18					
Total points					

Question 9—Why Trade?

People trade for many reasons, some rational and some irrational. Find two that make logical sense.

1. You need a challenge and adventure.

2. You want to make more money than is available from riskless investments.

3. You feel fed up with your day job.

4. You are more intelligent than most people you meet.

5. You want to make money.

A. 1 and 3

B. 4 and 5

C. 2 and 5

D. 2 and 3

Question 10—Trading Psychology

Match each statement to the type of trader who makes it.

1. My broker said this stock always goes up 3 or 4 points before a split.

2. My advisor's model portfolio was up 45% last year—how high did yours go?

3. Who knew the Feds would hit the market with a rate hike?

4. This stock is the lowest it's been in two years; it can't go any lower.

A. Practicing wishful thinking

B. Getting ready to blame the guru

C. Sideswiped by the news

Question 11—Causes of Losing

What are the main causes of traders' mortality?

1. Ignorance

2. Self-destructiveness

3. Undercapitalization

4. Bad advice

A. 1

B. 1 and 2

C. 1, 2, and 3

D. All of the above

Question 12—Alcoholics and Losers

The similarities between alcoholics and losers include all of the following, except:

1. They refuse to face the fact that they are drunks or losers.

2. They are not aware of how much they drink or lose.

3. They usually suffer from digestive problems and impotence.

4. They can benefit from an intervention by family and friends.

Question 13—Businessman's Risk

There are differences as well as similarities between a businessman's risk and loss. Which of the following phrases describe one or another, both or neither?

1. Destroys equity in the account

2. Comes unexpectedly

3. Determined by the percentage of account

4. No impact on a trader's survival

A. Businessman's risk

B. Loss

C. Both

D. Neither

Question 14—Pro's and Con's of Trading

All of the following phrases apply to trading, except for two:

1. Has a high entertainment value
2. Leads to winning if one finds the secret of trading success
3. Is a dangerous battle
4. Offers better odds than most games
5. Is an attractive part-time pursuit

A. 1 and 4
B. 2 and 5
C. 2 and 3
D. 3 and 5

Question 15—Trading Attitude

A mature trader:

1. Makes his own decisions
2. Accepts full responsibility for his losses
3. Can stand apart from the market crowd
4. Has an action plan for every market situation
5. Readily shares his knowledge and expertise

A. 1
B. 1 and 2
C. 1, 2, and 3
D. 1, 2, 3, and 4
E. All of the above

Question 16—Discipline

Disciplined trading means:

1. Having written rules for buying and selling

2. Testing rules for profit taking and stop-losses on historical data in the market you trade

3. Having a thorough record-keeping system for all trades

4. Reviewing prices of stocks on your watch list daily, whether you trade them or not

5. Not discussing your open positions with anyone

A. 1

B. 1 and 2

C. 1, 2, and 3

D. 1, 2, 3, and 4

E. All of the above

Question 17—Records

Match each phrase about keeping records with the items on the following page.

1. Turns a spotlight on problems and achievements

2. Keeps track of entries and exits, slippage and commissions

3. Keeping all your records up to date

4. Tracks the value of your account

5. Saves marked-up charts of entries and exits

A. Trader's diary

B. Equity curve

C. Outcome of record keeping

D. Trader's spreadsheet

E. Test of discipline

Question 18—Learning to Trade

Learning to trade is a lengthy process. Pick a pair of correct statements about it.

1. Having a large account leads to sloppy trading by beginners.

2. The more markets you trade, the faster you learn.

3. Feeling excited about a trade is a sign that it is likely to be profitable.

4. It pays to grade your performance on every trade.

5. Making money is more important that learning how to trade.

A. 1 and 3

B. 3 and 5

C. 3 and 4

D. 2 and 5

E. 1 and 4

BASIC CHARTING

Trading without charts is like playing poker without looking at the cards. It is important to learn to read charts because they can tell you a great deal about the never-ending battle between bulls and bears. If you want to track their moves, you have to be able to read their footprints on your charts.

Two city slickers go for a walk in the woods, and one says, "Look, there are bear tracks." "Don't be silly," says the other, "those are bull tracks." And that's when the train hit them. Anyone can see the tracks, but it takes knowledge and experience to recognize to whom they belong.

Once you learn to recognize price patterns in the middle of a chart, start shifting your attention to the right edge. The middle is where you learn, the right edge is where you trade. Making decisions at the right edge means acting while the information is not yet complete. Being able to recognize the picture from just a few details is a hallmark of a professional trader. It is also the reason why automatic trading tends not to work. Machines are not as good as humans when it comes to making decisions on the basis of incomplete information. Needless to say, your risk control has to be very good to allow you to act at the right edge.

Questions	Trial 1	Trial 2	Trial 3	Trial 4	Trial 5
19					
20					
21					
22					
23					
Total points					

Question 19—Prices

All of the following statements about price are correct, except:

1. What buyers are willing to pay

2. What sellers are willing to accept

3. A momentary consensus of value

4. A mirror image of values

5. Traders on the sidelines are irrelevant

A. 1 and 2

B. 3 and 4

C. 4 and 5

Question 20—A Bar Chart

Match the following price points of any bar with the statements on the following page.

1. High

2. Low

3. Open

4. Close

A. Maximum power of bears during that bar

B. More likely to represent amateurs' opinions on daily and weekly charts

C. Maximum power of bulls during that bar

D. More likely to represent professionals' opinions on daily and weekly charts

Question 21—Basic Charting

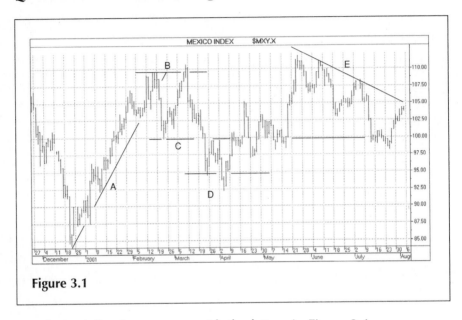

Figure 3.1

Match the following patterns with the letters in Figure 3.1.

1. Support

2. Resistance

3. Uptrendline

4. Downtrendline

5. Double top with a false breakout

6. Double bottom with a false breakout

And for extra credit:
At the right edge of the chart, bullish, bearish, or neutral? Please explain.

Question 22—Basic Charting

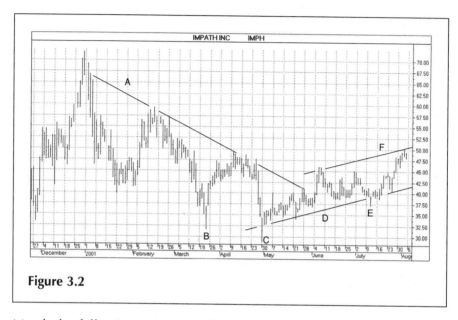

Figure 3.2

Match the following patterns with the letters in Figure 3.2:

1. Uptrendline

2. Downtrendline

3. Tail (kangaroo tail)

4. Channel line

And for extra credit:
At the right edge of the chart, bullish, bearish, or neutral? Please explain.

Question 23—Basic Charting

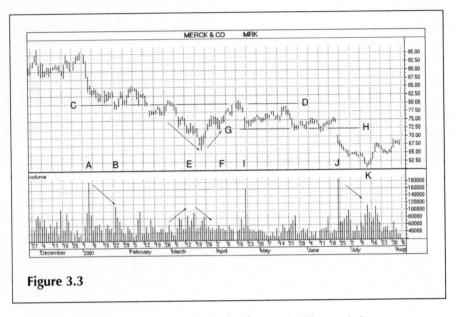

Figure 3.3

Match the following patterns with the letters in Figure 3.3:

1. Support/resistance

2. Volume spike

3. Increasing volume confirming trend

4. Falling volume indicating weak trend

5. Divergence

And for extra credit:
At the right edge of the chart, bullish, bearish, or neutral? Please explain.

INDICATORS—
FIVE BULLETS TO A CLIP

Why walk if you can drive? Why dig with a pick and shovel if an excavator is available? Modern computerized analysis allows traders to review more markets in greater depth and make more objective decisions than classical charting.

Computerized analysis does not guarantee success any more than having modern construction equipment guarantees building a sturdy house. You have to know how to use your tools. Draw the line between magic—buying someone else's collection of tools and hoping for a profitable outcome—and your own work of digging for good trading ideas using modern computerized tools.

A modern laptop packs more power than the first computers, which required special air-conditioned rooms and teams of service technicians. Modern technical analysis software is growing cheaper and more powerful each month. A serious trader owes it to himself to learn computerized analysis, whose primary tools are technical indicators.

Questions	Trial 1	Trial 2	Trial 3	Trial 4	Trial 5
24					
25					
26					
27					
28					
29					
30					
31					
32					
33					
34					
35					
36					
37					
38					
39					
Total points					

Question 24—Software

Which of the following phrases apply to toolbox software and which to black box software?

1. Includes undisclosed trading rules

2. Requires data entry

3. Assures profits if their rules are followed

4. Helps reveal the balance of power between bulls and bears

A. Toolbox

B. Black box

C. Both

D. Neither

Question 25—Indicators

Trend-following indicators help identify trends by showing that the market is moving in a certain direction with a certain inertia. Oscillators help identify reversal areas by showing when markets become overbought or oversold. Which of the following indicators belong to which group?

1. Moving average

2. MACD-Histogram

3. Stochastic

4. MACD-Lines

5. Force Index

A. Trend-following indicators

B. Oscillators

Question 26—Time

Which of the following statements about time in the markets are true and which are false?

1. The messages of a daily chart are more important than those of a weekly chart.

2. Analyzing multiple timeframes is essential for deep market analysis.

3. A day-trader needs a weekly chart.

4. Strategic decisions are made on short-term charts.

5. If rallies last longer than declines, they indicate that bulls are stronger.

A. True

B. False

Question 27—Moving Averages

Match the following phrases about moving averages (MAs):

1. The single most important message of an MA

2. An MA of (high + low + close) / 3

3. Using a longer time window for an MA

4. Assigning a lesser role to old data

5. Buying in the vicinity of a rising MA

A. Especially useful for day-traders

B. Reduces whipsaws

C. A value trade

D. The slope of an MA

E. An exponential MA

Question 28—Moving Averages

Match the following patterns with the letters in Figure 4.1:

1. Uptrend

2. Downtrend

3. Value buy

4. Greater fool theory buy

5. Value short

6. Kangaroo tail

7. Double bottom

And for extra credit:
At the right edge of the chart, bullish, bearish, or neutral? Please explain.

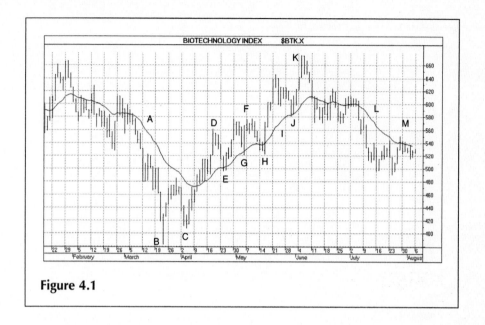

Figure 4.1

Question 29—Channels

Match the following phrases about channels:

1. The normal limit of optimism

2. Contains approximately 95% of recent prices

3. Must fit market extremes in a bear market

4. The longer it is, the wider the channel

5. Becomes wider when market grows more volatile

A. Envelope

B. Bollinger bands

C. Lower channel line

D. Market timeframe

E. Upper channel line

Question 30—Channels

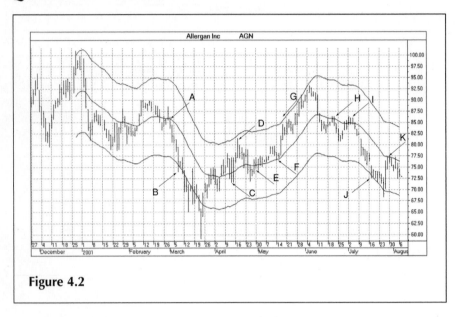

Figure 4.2

Match the following channel signals with the letters in Figure 4.2:

1. Buy

2. Sell, take profits

3. Sell short

4. Cover shorts

And for extra credit:
At the right edge of the chart, bullish, bearish, or neutral? Please explain.

Question 31—Grading Trades

Envelopes or channels can help you grade your performance as a trader. What are the grades for the following trades:

1. Trader A buys a stock at 56, above the rising EMA, and sells at 59. The upper line is at 60.5, the lower at 49.5.

2. Trader B buys a stock 17.5, near the rising EMA, and sells at 18.5. The upper channel line is at 20, the lower at 13.

3. Trader C buys a stock in a trading range at 21, but it sinks and he bails out on a stop at 19. The upper line is at 24, the lower at 16.

4. Trader D sells short a stock at 88, near a falling moving average, and covers at 81. The upper line is at 99, the lower at 81.

Question 32—MACD

Match the following phrases about MACD:

1. Long-term consensus of value

2. MACD-Histogram

3. Short-term consensus of value

4. Lower peak of MACD-Histogram while prices reach a higher peak

5. Higher bottom of MACD-Histogram while prices sink to a lower low

A. Fast line of MACD

B. Bullish divergence

C. Bearish divergence

D. Slow line of MACD

E. The spread between MACD-lines

Question 33—MACD

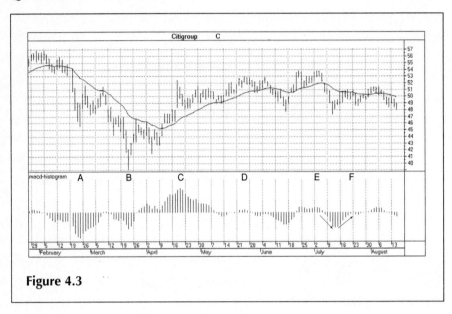

Figure 4.3

Match the following signals of MACD-Histogram with the letters in Figure 4.3:

1. Uptrend

2. Downtrend

3. Bullish divergence

4. Bearish divergence

5. Price tail

And for extra credit:
At the right edge of the chart, bullish, bearish, or neutral? Please explain.

Question 34—Force Index

Which of the following phrases does not apply to Force Index?

1. Measures price changes

2. Depends on the direction of prices

3. Should be smoothed with an EMA

4. Measures day-to-day volume changes

5. Spikes tend to mark reversal areas

Question 35—Force Index

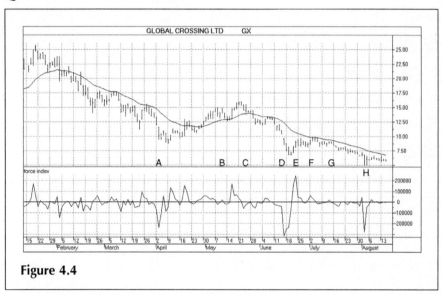

Figure 4.4

Match the following signals of Force Index with the letters in Figure 4.4:

1. Buy signal

2. Sell signal

3. Bullish divergence

4. Spike

And for extra credit:
At the right edge of the chart, bullish, bearish, or neutral? Please explain.

Question 36—Elder-ray

Match the following statements about Elder-ray:

1. Bear Power becoming negative, then ticking up

2. The distance from the high of the bar to the EMA

3. The average consensus of value

4. The distance from the low of the bar to the EMA

5. Bull Power becoming positive, then ticking down

A. Moving average

B. Sell signal in a downtrend

C. Bear Power

D. Buy signal during an uptrend

E. Bull Power

Question 37—Elder-ray

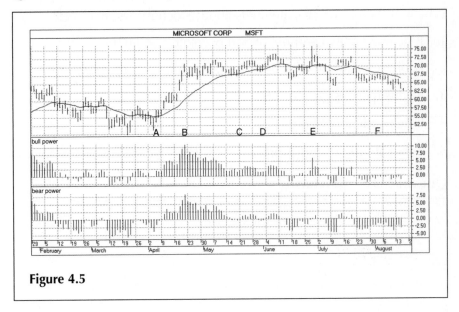

Figure 4.5

Match the following signals of Elder-ray with the letters in Figure 4.5:

1. Buy signal from Bear Power

2. Shorting signal from Bull Power

3. New peak of Bull Power—expect higher prices ahead

4. Bearish divergence of Bull Power

5. Price tail

And for extra credit:
At the right edge of the chart, bullish, bearish, or neutral? Please explain.

Question 38—Stochastic

Which of the following statements about Stochastic is incorrect?

1. It helps identify overbought and oversold conditions.

2. Look to sell when Stochastic is above its upper reference line.

3. Its divergences give the strongest signals.

4. It helps identify trends.

5. Avoid shorting when Stochastic is below its lower reference line.

Question 39—Stochastic

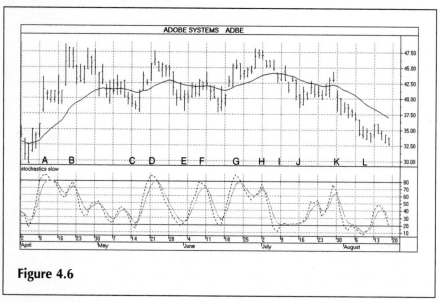

Figure 4.6

Match the following Stochastic signals with the letters in Figure 4.6:

1. Buy signal

2. Sell signal

3. Bullish divergence

4. Bearish divergence

And for extra credit:
At the right edge of the chart, bullish, bearish, or neutral? Please explain.

TRADING

Beginning traders tend to stumble into several pitfalls. Many jump into the markets without knowing enough about trading. Some make a few dollars thanks to beginners' luck, but practically all beginners end up losing money. That's when they hit the books—and more and more books, afraid to pull the trigger, with lingering memories of the beating they received. A beaten trader who concentrates on market analysis but does not trade is suffering from "paralysis from analysis."

An intelligent trader realizes that his or her knowledge of the market can never be complete. The markets are huge, influenced by many factors, and have a fair bit of uncertainty. There is no such thing as perfect understanding. Once the preponderance of signals from your indicators points to a trade, it is time to calculate the risks, set stops, and put on the trade, without waiting for a perfect signal, which is likely to come too late anyway.

Questions	Trial 1	Trial 2	Trial 3	Trial 4	Trial 5
40					
41					
42					
43					
44					
45					
46					
47					
Total points					

Question 40—Systems

Which of the following statements about trading systems are true?

1. Trading systems help reduce the volume of market information to a few key factors.

2. A discretionary trader uses somewhat different tools at different times.

3. Exits are more important than entries in designing systems.

4. Systems parameters must be changed with the passage of time.

5. A good system could be automated and given to someone else to trade.

A. 1

B. 1 and 2

C. 1, 2, and 3

D. 1, 2, 3, and 4

E. All of the above

Question 41—System Testing

Which of the following statements about testing systems are true?

1. A valid system provides an expectation of profits greater than losses.

2. A computerized test of a system is more objective than manually clicking forward one day at a time.

3. Manual testing imitates the psychological stresses of trading.

4. Money management rules can be ignored if testing shows that trading without them will lead to better performance.

5. A system bought from a reputable vendor who thoroughly tested it can be put immediately to work.

A. 1

B. 1 and 2

C. 1, 2, and 3

D. 1, 2, 3, and 4

E. All of the above

Question 42—Paper Trading

Which of the following statements about paper trading are true?

1. People tend to be less emotional when paper trading.

2. Most paper traders are those who have become afraid of actual trading after losing money.

3. The best reason to paper trade is to test your discipline.

4. Homework for paper trading takes less time than for real trading.

5. The profit and loss of real trading tends to follow that of paper trading.

A. 1

B. 1 and 2

C. 1, 2, and 3

D. 1, 2, 3, and 4

E. All of the above

Question 43—Indicators

Match the following phrases on technical indicators:

1. Bullish consensus, new high–new low index

2. More objective than chart patterns

3. Moving averages, MACD-Lines, Directional System

4. Often in conflict with other groups of indicators

5. Envelopes, Force Index, Stochastic, Elder-ray

A. Trend-following

B. Oscillators

C. Miscellaneous

D. All indicators

Question 44—Timeframes

Which of the following statements about market timeframes are true?

1. The factor of five connects all timeframes.

2. Indicator signals in different timeframes often contradict one another.

3. Intraday charts allow you to get closer to the market than daily charts.

4. The definition of long term is derived from the intermediate-term charts.

5. It is important to look at short-term charts before reviewing long-term charts.

A. 1

B. 1 and 2

C. 1, 2, and 3

D. 1, 2, 3, and 4

E. All of the above

Question 45—Triple Screen

Which sequence of phrases best describes Triple Screen?

1. Strategic decision on the daily, tactical on the weekly, execution intraday

2. Strategic decision intraday, tactical on the weekly, execution daily

3. Strategic decision on the weekly, tactical on the daily, execution intraday

4. Strategic decision on the daily, tactical intraday, execution weekly

5. Strategic decision intraday, tactical on the daily, execution weekly

Question 46—Entering Trades

All of the following entry methods are acceptable, except:

1. Buy on a breakout above yesterday's high.

2. Buy on a pullback to the EMA.

3. Use intraday charts to buy pullbacks.

4. Place a market order to buy before the opening.

5. Buy when Force Index becomes negative.

Question 47—Taking Profits

Which of the following signals are appropriate for taking profits on long positions?

1. Prices hit the upper channel line.

2. The two-day EMA of Force Index spikes up.

3. The EMA turns from up to flat.

4. Prices approach overhead resistance.

5. You are afraid that the market will reverse.

A. 1

B. 1 and 2

C. 1, 2, and 3

D. 1, 2, 3, and 4

E. All of the above

DAY-TRADING

Day-trading is much harder than most people think. Beginners stumbling into this field usually get the same financial result as from playing three-card monte on the street. The cards get shuffled a little too fast, the expense of getting in and out is a little too high, the player's attention flags just a little, and soon another day-trading wannabe bites the dust.

Day-trading demands instant reactions and the highest degree of discipline, but, paradoxically, tends to attract the most impulsive and hyperactive people. It demands a total concentration on short-term swings, and most people simply cannot focus their attention long enough.

Still, day-trading has its uses, even for longer-term traders. If you know how to day-trade, you can use those techniques to slide into and out of your positions. Once you do that, turn off your real-time screen and focus on longer-term charts. Be sure to keep the two types of trading apart—do not convert position trades into day-trades and vice versa.

Questions	Trial 1	Trial 2	Trial 3	Trial 4	Trial 5
48					
49					
50					
51					
52					
53					
Total points					

Question 48—Day-Trading Challenges

Which of the following challenges are unique to day-trading?

1. Profits per trade are smaller, because of shorter swings.

2. Expenses are higher, because of more frequent trading.

3. Traders must act instantly or wash out.

4. It is more time-consuming than position trading.

5. Losing trades are bigger than with position trading.

A. 1

B. 1 and 2

C. 1, 2, and 3

D. 1, 2, 3, and 4

E. All of the above

Question 49—Day-Trading Psychology

Which two of the following statements on day-trading psychology are incorrect?

1. Day-trading demands less attention than position trading.

2. Day-traders trade for reasons that are partly rational and partly irrational.

3. Day-trading plays into people's addictive streaks.

4. Day-trading generates less income for brokers than position trading.

5. Having a written plan is a sign of disciplined day-trading.

A. 1 and 3

B. 2 and 5

C. 1 and 4

D. 3 and 4

E. 2 and 3

Question 50—Day-Trading

You may scan all of the following lists for day-trading candidates, except:

1. Most popular technology stocks

2. Most promising penny stocks

3. Blue chips

4. 20 most active on the NASDAQ

5. 20 most active on the NYSE

Question 51—Opening Ranges

Match the following statements:

1. Professionals accommodate outsiders eager to enter the market.

2. A breakout from this opening range is not likely to last.

3. These bars tend to have the lowest trading volume.

4. Professionals let outsiders get out by taking their unwanted stocks.

5. The opening range is likely to lead to an important breakout.

A. Narrow opening range

B. The last half-hour of trading

C. The middle of the day

D. The first half-hour of trading

E. Wide opening range

Question 52—Day-Trading

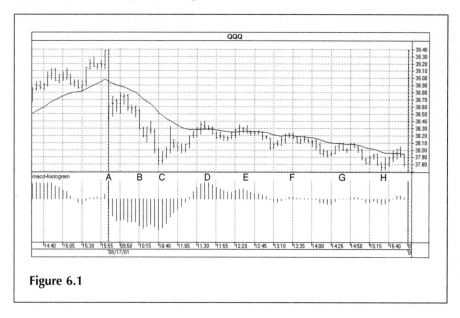

Figure 6.1

The 25-minute chart (not shown) is in a downtrend. Please review the five-minute chart in Figure 6.1 and match the following signals with the letters in the chart. Thick vertical bars mark the beginning and the end of each trading session.

1. Breakout from the opening range

2. Downward gap

3. Shorting signal

4. New extreme of bears' strength

5. Bullish divergence

And for extra credit:
At the right edge of the chart, bullish, bearish, or neutral? Please explain.

Question 53—The Daily Plan

Which of the following statements about the daily plan are correct?

1. You should start working before the opening bell.

2. Stocks on your monitoring list must be reviewed more than once a day.

3. It is OK to listen to trading tips as long as you filter them through your system.

4. Trading in a room full of people leads to more objective decisions.

5. It is better not to plan what you will trade, but choose after the market opens.

A. 1

B. 1 and 2

C. 1, 2, and 3

D. 1, 2, 3, and 4

E. All of the above

ADVANCED CONCEPTS

To succeed in trading, you need an advantage over your competitors. The best edge is a very high level of discipline. Another good edge comes from a deeper level of understanding of the markets. This is usually based on having unusual and original analytic tools, that are not available to the mass of traders.

Successful traders tend to rely on private tools and techniques, or else they use commonly known tools in uncommon ways. Here we will review two new methods—the Impulse System for finding trades and SafeZone for placing stops. We will also look at the derivatives— options and futures. A beginner is better off staying away from them and learning to trade stocks, but an experienced trader may expand his area of interest to include derivatives.

Questions	Trial 1	Trial 2	Trial 3	Trial 4	Trial 5
54					
55					
56					
57					
58					
59					
60					
61					
62					
63					
64					
65					
66					
67					
Total points					

Question 54—The Impulse System

Match the following phrases regarding the Impulse System:

1. The hardest thing about momentum trading

2. Reflects growing bullish momentum

3. Reflects bearish inertia

4. Reflects growing bearish momentum

5. Reflects bullish inertia

6. Waiting for confirmation

A. Rising EMA

B. Rising MACD-Histogram

C. Reduces the profitability of a trade

D. Falling EMA

E. Knowing when to jump out of a trade

F. Falling MACD-Histogram

Question 55—The Impulse System

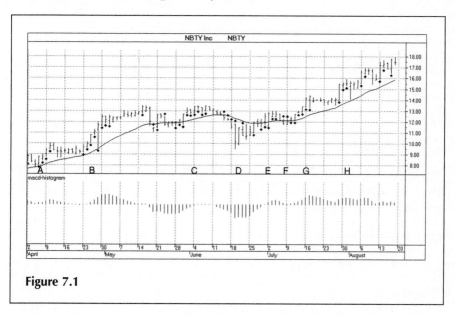

Figure 7.1

The weekly chart is in an uptrend. Please review the daily chart in Figure 7.1 and match the following signals with the letters in the chart.

1. Cluster of sell signals

2. Cluster of buy signals

And for extra credit:
At the right edge of the chart, bullish, bearish, or neutral? Please explain.

Question 56—The Impulse System

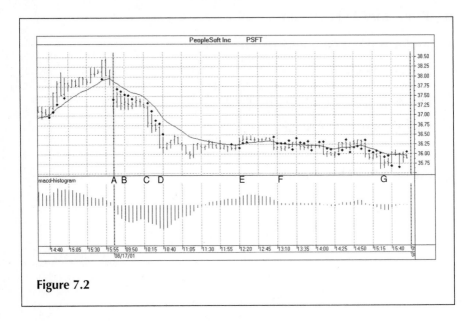

Figure 7.2

The 25-minute chart (not shown) is in a downtrend. Please review the five-minute chart in Figure 7.2 and match the following signals with the letters in the chart. Thick vertical bars mark the beginning and the end of each trading session.

1. Cluster of buy signals

2. Cluster of sell signals

3. Downward gap

4. Breakout from the opening range

5. New extreme of bears' strength

6. Bullish divergence

And for extra credit:
At the right edge of the chart, bullish, bearish, or neutral? Please explain.

Question 57—Exits

Which of the following statements about exits are correct?

1. Weigh risks and rewards by comparing the distances from the entrance to the profit target and then to a stop level.

2. Traders tend to be more objective about exits before entering a trade.

3. The distance to the stop should be larger than that to the profit target.

4. The best time to plan an exit is when you are in the trade.

5. Once in place, the profit target never shifts.

A. 1

B. 1 and 2

C. 1, 2, and 3

D. 1, 2, 3, and 4

E. All of the above

Question 58—Exits

Which of the following statements on using channels for exits are correct?

1. Prices of securities always oscillate above and below value.

2. The wider the channel, the more attractive the trade.

3. Channels help traders sell above value and cover shorts at depressed levels.

4. A well-drawn channel will nail down essentially all tops and bottoms.

5. A well-drawn channel contains 99% of prices for the past few months.

A. 1

B. 1 and 2

C. 1, 2, and 3

D. 1, 2, 3, and 4

E. All of the above

Question 59—Exits

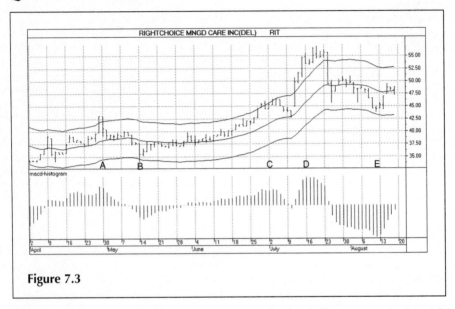

Figure 7.3

Review the chart in Figure 7.3 and match the following signals with the letters in the chart.

1. Take profits on longs

2. Take profits on shorts

And for extra credit:
At the right edge of the chart, bullish, bearish, or neutral? Please explain.

Question 60—Stops

Which of the following statements regarding stops are true and which are false?

1. The time to place a stop is immediately after entering a trade.

2. Superior market analysis makes stops unnecessary.

3. Mental stops are safer than those placed in the market.

4. Stops must be linked with money management rules.

5. Stops are defined by technical analysis.

Question 61—SafeZone

Match the following phrases and statements regarding SafeZone stops:

1. The trend is up; market noise is defined by....

2. Multiply the Average Upside Penetration by a coefficient and add it to the high.

3. The trend is down; market noise is defined by....

4. Average Downside Penetration during the lookback period.

5. Multiply the Average Downside Penetration by a coefficient and deduct it from the low.

6. Average Upside Penetration during the lookback period.

A. SafeZone stop in an uptrend

B. The extent by which today's low is deeper than yesterday's low

C. Average noise level in an uptrend

D. The extent by which today's high exceeds yesterday's high

E. SafeZone stop in a downtrend

F. Average noise level in a downtrend

Question 62—Trading on Margin

Which of the following statements about trading stocks on margin are correct?

1. Allows you to leverage your buying power
2. Leads to greater losses on losing trades
3. More stressful than cash trades
4. Allows you to make bigger profits from correct decisions
5. Helps small traders make more profits and grow equity

A. 1

B. 1 and 2

C. 1, 2, and 3

D. 1, 2, 3, and 4

E. All of the above

Question 63—Trends and Swings

Which of the following statements apply to trend trading and which to swing trading?

1. Channel width is relatively unimportant.
2. They are easy to trade.
3. You need to give trades some extra room with stops.
4. It is often done with the most active stocks.
5. Take profits at the channel line.

A. Trend trading

B. Swing trading

C. Neither

Question 64—Options

Option prices depend on all of the following, except:

1. Their distance to the exercise price

2. Their time to the expiration

3. Market trend

4. Interest rates

5. Stock volatility

Question 65—Options

With a stock trading at 65 in March, an options trader has several choices. Match each choice with the position it describes:

1. Buy stock and sell 70 May call

2. Buy 60 May put

3. Sell 60 May put

4. Buy 60 May call and sell 60 July–May call

5. Buy 70 May call

A. Naked write

B. Covered write

C. Spread trade

D. Long call

E. Long put

Question 66—Options

Which of the following statements about option writing are correct?

1. Money management is the key requirement for writing options.
2. Writing naked options leads to limited reward with unlimited risk.
3. It is better to write puts when you are bullish.
4. A writer must wait for the expiration date to take profits.
5. Time is the enemy of the option writer.

A. 1
B. 1 and 2
C. 1, 2, and 3
D. 1, 2, 3, and 4
E. All of the above

Question 67—Futures

Match the following phrases regarding futures:

1. Taking a position in futures opposite to one's position in the actual commodity
2. The main source of risk in futures
3. Nearby months selling for more than faraway months
4. Industrial producers and consumers
5. Severe weather in production areas

A. Inverted market
B. Inside information
C. Supply-driven market
D. Hedging
E. Low margin requirements

MONEY MANAGEMENT

The third M of successful trading, Money, is certainly the most neglected. Beginners spend a lot of time and energy trying to learn Methods, and more experienced traders worry about their discipline and other topics of the Mind, but only the pros pay enough attention to Money.

A professional understands that whether he trades an Internet high-flyer, soybean futures, or IBM calls, he is ultimately trading money. Any specific market is just a vehicle that may bring him a higher return than a bank. This is why counting money is no less important—perhaps more important—than counting indicator readings.

Have you noticed how, in trading, everything that can go wrong tends to go wrong? There are legions of people making a living in the markets, and they make money when you stumble. Every imaginable banana peel gets thrown in your path. To protect yourself from losses, you need to establish and religiously observe money management rules.

Money management provides a safety net on your journey to that appealing land where you will be free because you trade for a living. If you have a reasonably good method for analyzing the markets and finding trades, you will succeed, if—and this is a very big if—you can protect your capital along the way.

To underscore the extreme importance of money management, your answers will be graded differently in this chapter. There will be no "fairly good" rating. You must obtain an Excellent score because the only other rating is Poor. Poor in more ways than one.

Questions	Trial 1	Trial 2	Trial 3	Trial 4	Trial 5
68					
69					
70					
71					
72					
73					
74					
75					
76					
77					
78					
79					
80					
81					
82					
Total points					

Question 68—Mathematical Expectation

A trading system has a positive mathematical expectation when it:

1. Makes money on most trades

2. Has more winning trades than losing

3. Guarantees profits

4. Works well without money management

5. Gives you an edge in the market

Question 69—Numerical Literacy

Test your arithmetic skills, calculate the answers in your head, and write down the answers:

1. 187 + 346

2. 12% of 200

3. 345 divided by 5

4. 37.5 multiplied by 500

5. The chance of snow is 25% on Saturday and 25% on Sunday. What is the chance of snow during the entire weekend?

Question 70—The 2% Rule

Following the 2% Rule means:

1. Buying no more than $2,000 worth of stock in a $100,000 account

2. Risking no less than $400 in a $20,000 account

3. Risking no more than $3,000 in a $150,000 account

4. Aiming for at least a $2,000 profit in a $100,000 account

5. Aiming for at least a $2 profit per share in a $100 stock

Question 71—The 2% Rule

Which of the following trades may be taken in a $50,000 account? (Remember, try to answer without a calculator.)

1. Buy 500 shares of a $25 stock, with a stop at $23.50

2. Sell short 300 shares of a $48 stock, with a stop at $51

3. Buy 1,000 shares of a $12 stock, with a stop at $11

4. Sell short 200 shares of a $92 stock, with a stop at $98

5. Buy 700 shares of a $33 stock, with a stop at $31

A. 1

B. 1 and 2

C. 1, 2, and 3

D. 1, 2, 3, and 4

E. All of the above

Question 72—Businessman's Risk

Which of the following exposes you to a businessman's risk and which to risk of a loss?

1. $100,000 account, buy 1,000 shares of a $50 stock, stop at $48.75

2. $20,000 account, buy 300 shares of a $30 stock, stop at $28

3. $20,000 account, buy 200 shares of a $20 stock, stop at $18.50

4. $100,000 account, buy 1,000 shares of a $40 stock, stop at $36

5. $100,000 account, buy 1,000 shares of a $50 stock, no stop

A. Businessman's risk

B. Risk of loss

Question 73—The 2% Rule

Bill is a beginning stock trader with a $25,000 account. He selects a $40 stock that he expects to rally to $48, and wants to place a stop at $36, below support. He wants to trade a round lot of 100 shares. Can he afford to take this trade?

Question 74—The 2% Rule

Gary is a beginning futures trader with $20,000 in his account. He wants to sell short gold, which he expects to fall by $9 per ounce. If gold rallies $3 per ounce, it will cancel his downtrend scenario and trigger a stop. There are 100 ounces of gold in each contract. Can he afford to take this trade?

Question 75—The 2% Rule

Susan is a stock trader with $50,000 in her account. She selects a $24 stock that she expects to rise to $30. She identifies support at $22 and wants to place a stop at $21.50. She plans to buy 500 shares. Can she afford to take this trade?

Question 76—Private and Institutional

The main reason institutional traders tend to do better than private traders is:

1. More capital

2. Built-in support network of other traders

3. Having a manager

4. Better training

5. Less stress trading other people's money

Question 77—The 6% Rule

Following the 6% Rule means:

1. Aim to make 6% profit per month in your account.

2. Stop trading for the rest of the month after losing 6% of equity.

3. Keep your profit/loss ratio at 6:2.

4. Close out all position after risk exceeds 6%.

5. Never have more than three open trades if you follow the 2% Rule.

Question 78—The 6% Rule

Ann starts the month with $90,000. She puts on trades A and B, risking $1,200 on each, and loses. She then puts on trades C and D, risking $1,500 on each, and moves stops on both to breakeven. Now she sees trade E and wants to buy 500 shares, risking $3 on each. May she take this trade?

Question 79—The 6% Rule

Peter starts the month with $150,000. He has several winning trades, and then loses $2,500 on each of two trades in a row. He now has two open trades of 1,000 shares each, with stops $1.90 and $1.70 away from his entry prices. He recognizes an extremely attractive trading opportunity on his screen. May he take it?

Question 80—The 6% Rule

Jim starts the month with $30,000. He puts on trades A, B, and C, risking $500 in each. Trades A and C reach his profit targets; trade B sinks and hits his stop. He sees potential trades D and E, with the risk of $500 on each of them. May he take them?

Question 81—Position Sizing

Which of the following statements are true and which are false?

1. The smaller the trade, relative to account size, the more likely it is to be profitable.

2. When losing, it is important to increase the size of trades to make back losses.

3. The amount of risk has a direct impact on the quality of trading decisions.

4. If you aim for big profits, survival will come naturally.

5. The amount at risk is more important than trade size in making decisions.

Question 82—Position Sizing

Which of the following is most indicative of overtrading in a $100,000 account?

1. Putting on three trades a day

2. Having 10 open positions with $750 risk in each

3. 10 trades a week

4. Trading 5,000-share lots

5. Having five open positions with $1,000 risk in each

THE ORGANIZED TRADER

If you have worked through this book so far, you appreciate that trading is a serious pursuit. It requires the utmost concentration, attention, and dedication. You may mean well, but how can you be sure that your actions follow your intentions? You want to avoid having to say, like a former Russian prime minister, "We wanted the best, but got the usual." Or, as my grandfather used to say, "The road to Hell is paved with good intentions."

The only way to tell whether you are on the right track is by keeping good notes. Show me a trader with good notes, and I will show you a good trader.

Keeping extensive records and reviewing them is a lot less fun than swinging in the markets, buying here and selling there. Good records provide the best running test of your level of discipline. If you score high on that test—not just in this book, but after you are finished working with it, in your own trading—you should do well and succeed in trading for a living.

Grading in this chapter, as in the Money Management chapter, is different from the rest of this book. This topic is so important that there is no "fairly good" rating. You must keep learning until you score Excellent.

Questions	Trial 1	Trial 2	Trial 3	Trial 4	Trial 5
83					
84					
85					
86					
87					
88					
89					
90					
91					
92					
93					
94					
95					
96					
97					
98					
99					
100					
Total points					

Question 83—Elements of Successful Trading*

Which of the following is the single most important factor in successful trading?

1. Intelligence

2. Experience

3. Discipline

4. Imagination

5. Training

Question 84—Trading Records

All of the following statements about keeping trading records are correct, except:

1. They are the best reflection of a trader's discipline.

2. Good records allow traders to be more relaxed with money management.

3. They are an essential factor in a trader's success and survival.

4. Good records prevent traders from repeating mistakes.

5. Good records improve traders' profit/loss ratios.

---

*Thanks to Robert Rotella, the title of whose book I borrowed to name this question.

Question 85—Trader's Spreadsheet

Which of the following records belong in a trader's spreadsheet?

1. Dates of entries and exits

2. Entry and exit prices

3. Commissions and fees

4. Performance grades

5. Entry and exit grades

A. 1

B. 1 and 2

C. 1, 2, and 3

D. 1, 2, 3, and 4

E. All of the above

Question 86—Trading Equity

Which of the following count as components of equity in your trading account?

1. Cash in your trading account

2. The total value of open trades

3. Treasury bills held in your trading account

4. Margin credit

5. Reserve savings

A. 1

B. 1 and 2

C. 1, 2, and 3

D. 1, 2, 3, and 4

E. All of the above

Question 87—Equity Curve

Five traders each start with a $100,000 account. Whose equity curve is more likely to draw the attention of fund managers?

1. End with $119,000, biggest drawdown $7,600

2. End with $98,000, biggest drawdown $4,100

3. End with $74,000, biggest drawdown $51,000

4. End with $134,000, biggest drawdown $28,000

5. End with $114,000, biggest drawdown $2,800

Question 88—Trading Diary

What is the optimal number of charts in a trading diary?

1. One for entry and one for exit

2. Two or three for entry and one for exit

3. One for entry and two or three for exit

4. Two or three for both entry and exit

5. Five or more for both entry and exit

Question 89—Trading Diary

Which of the following phrases about a trading diary are correct?

1. Allows you to learn from mistakes and successes

2. Reduces the emotionalism in trading

3. Serves as a precise indicator of your discipline

4. Must be done for every trade

5. Should be done for the most interesting trades

A. 1

B. 1 and 2

C. 1, 2, and 3

D. 1, 2, 3, and 4

E. All of the above

Question 90—Entry and Exit Grades

A trader buys a stock at 47 on the day when the high is 48 and the low is 44. He sells it a few days later at 51, on the day when the high is 54 and the low 50. What is his entry grade for this trade? What is his exit grade?

1. 0%

2. 25%

3. 50%

4. 75%

5. 100%

Question 91—Trading Decisions

Why is it easier to make trading decisions when the markets are closed?

1. The opportunity to pause, think, and return to your charts later for another look
2. Lack of pressure from prices moving while you analyze them
3. The ability to compare your stock with many other stocks and indexes
4. The ability to review advisory newsletters
5. The ability to ask other traders for advice

A. 1

B. 1 and 2

C. 1, 2, and 3

D. 1, 2, 3, and 4

E. All of the above

Question 92—Action Plan

Match the following phrases about an action plan:

1. Writing down chart descriptions
2. Writing down what to do in the day ahead
3. Writing descriptions before plans
4. Reading from a sheet while placing orders
5. Specifying your trading size

A. Having to explain what factors led to a trading decision

B. Planning while the market is closed

C. Being clear on facts before moving to their interpretations

D. Adhering to your money management discipline

E. Avoiding emotional mistakes while placing orders

Question 93—Trading Records

Which of the following records are essential for successful trading?

1. Trader's spreadsheet

2. Equity curve

3. Trading diary

4. Action plan

5. ABC rating system

A. 1

B. 1 and 2

C. 1, 2, and 3

D. 1, 2, 3, and 4

E. All of the above

Question 94—Second-Guessing Systems

Second-guessing a trading system:

1. Leads to decisions not ordered by the system

2. Increases the range of choices available to a trader

3. Improves the chances of success

4. Is a sign of psychological strength

5. Leads to more disciplined trading

A. 1

B. 1 and 2

C. 1, 2, and 3

D. 1, 2, 3, and 4

E. All of the above

Question 95—Disclosing Trades

Talking about open positions:

1. Invites advice from other traders

2. Makes you more popular with other traders

3. Helps you see options you have not considered

4. Increases the likelihood of a successful trade

5. Increases the likelihood of long-term success

A. 1

B. 1 and 2

C. 1, 2, and 3

D. 1, 2, 3, and 4

E. All of the above

Question 96—Time Management

Managing time while trading financial markets involves:

1. A weekly review of all markets in which you have any interest

2. A daily review of all markets in which you have open positions

3. Preparing a timetable of earnings reports for the stocks you own

4. Watching the openings of all markets you consider entering

5. Watching the closings of all markets you consider exiting

A. 1

B. 1 and 2

C. 1, 2, and 3

D. 1, 2, 3, and 4

E. All of the above

Question 97—The ABC Rating System

Match the following phrases about the ABC rating system:

1. May trade this market tomorrow

2. A quick overview of all markets

3. Not likely to trade this market this week

4. An in-depth review of a few markets

5. May trade this market in a few days

A. Group A

B. Group B

C. Group C

D. Done daily

E. Done weekly

Question 98—The Decision-Making Tree

Which of the following combinations fits most closely with a discretionary trader's decision-making tree?

1. Flexible analytic rules, flexible use of multiple timeframes, flexible money management rules

2. Strict analytic rules, strict use of multiple timeframes, strict money management rules

3. Strict analytic rules, strict use of multiple timeframes, flexible money management rules

4. Flexible analytic rules, flexible use of multiple timeframes, strict money management rules

5. Flexible analytic rules, strict use of multiple timeframes, flexible money management rules

Question 99—Trading Priorities

Which of the following best describes the order of priorities for a serious trader?

1. Extraordinary profits, steady profits, survival

2. Survival, steady profits, extraordinary profits

3. Steady profits, extraordinary profits, survival

4. Survival, extraordinary profits, steady profits

5. Extraordinary profits, survival, steady profits

Question 100—Trading Career

What is the best sequence for developing a long-term trading plan?

1. Develop a decision-making tree, set money management rules, keep records

2. Keep records, develop a decision-making tree, set money management rules

3. Set money management rules, keep records, develop a decision-making tree

4. Develop a decision-making tree, keep records, set money management rules

5. Keep records, set money management rules, develop a decision-making tree

ANSWERS AND RATING SCALES

FINANCIAL TRADING FOR BABES IN THE WOODS

Answer 1

A. 2, 6

B. 3, 5

C. 1, 4

Give yourself a point for each correct answer.

Researching a stock's prospects and its industry group is a hallmark of a serious investor. An insider is the ultimate investor, albeit a criminal, because he is acting on a fundamental factor likely to move a stock. The closeness of insider trading to fundamental analysis is an endless source of embarrassment for many brokerage firms. A trader focuses on the response of prices to the fundamental data, including mass hysteria. A gambler who gets his tips from some famous guru on TV is still a gambler because he chases hot leads instead of thinking for himself.

Answer 2

True. 2, 5

False. 1, 3, 4

Give yourself a point for each correct answer.

Traders often focus on feelings rather than maximizing profits. A trader who buys a runaway stock out of fear of missing a good thing is hardly being rational. Professionals do not expect to win in every trade and are aware of a great deal of noise and uncertainty in the markets; they do expect to be profitable in the long run, thanks to steady disciplined trading. When a group agrees that a certain trade looks good, it is usually time to go the other way because groups tend to be more emotional than individuals. Boiling markets are less rational, creating opportunities for calm pros; quiet markets are more efficient, making it more difficult to take money from others.

Answer 3

1. E

2. D

3. B

4. C

5. A

Give yourself a point for each correct answer, with a bonus point if you got #4 right.

Any fool can enter a trade (and often does), but it takes knowledge and experience to find good exit points. Entries have to be planned in advance. An intelligent trader decides he will enter after the market does what he expects it to do, and then waits for all his ducks to get in a row. A momentum trader tries to catch an impulse move, a countertrend trader a return to value; both methods can be profitable, as long as you know clearly what it is you are trying to do each time. While analyzing prices and indicators, you should not forget that money management is the essential element of trading; each trade has to be chosen in accordance with strict money management rules.

Answer 4

1. C

2. A

3. A, B, C

4. B, C

5. A, B, C

Give yourself a point for each completely correct answer.

Options are deadly for most buyers who must jump through three hoops, correctly choosing the vehicle, price, and time. A stock makes you a part owner of a business, whereas both futures and options deal in contracts for future delivery and allow you to get out of your commitment before the due date. A trader with no money management skills will lose in every market, but his loss will come sooner in options or futures than in stocks. The trend is your friend in every market; there is no point in buying when prices are falling.

Answer 5

1. A, B, C

2. C

3. B

4. D

5. A

Give yourself a point for each completely correct answer.

Dripping water shapes mountains, and commissions, slippage, and expenses shape traders' accounts, affecting them more in the long run than most trades. Commissions are set by brokers, and slippage can often be avoided, but expenses can be controlled by traders. Slippage is the distance between the market order and the transaction price; it is small in quiet markets, greater in boiling markets. No expense is meaningless—they all raise barriers to your success. Commissions and, at times, slippage are what you pay for the privilege of entering a trading arena, and their combination cannot be reduced below a certain minimum.

Answer 6

5. Give yourself five points for choosing the correct answer.

An important survival factor is the maximum percentage of the account risked on any given trade. It would take a string of 50 losses to knock traders 4 and 5 out of the game, but a mere five losses can dispatch trader 3. A bigger account offers several advantages: the cost of services eats up a smaller percentage and diversification is easier.

Answer 7

C. 3 and 4. Give yourself five points for choosing the correct answer, or two points if you answered B (one correct out of two).

Earnings are important, but the market's reaction to them is even more telling. When a stock refuses to decline after a bad earnings report, it shows that the bottom is near. A steep drop after a mildly disappointing earnings report indicates further weakness ahead. Futures can fall below the cost of production when desperate producers dump their overstock, but they cannot stay there for long. Real-time data only distracts beginners, as does watching a multitude of markets. Weekly charts provide the essential long-term perspective, while the best software in the hands of a yahoo is useless because knowledge and skills carry more weight than any tools.

Answer 8

A. 1

B. 3

C. 5

D. 2, 4

Give yourself a point for each correct answer.

Fundamental analysts study supply and demand, which drive prices in the long run. Market technicians try to read the behavior of the market crowd. Both can be used for making trading decisions, although fundamentals are more important for long-term investors and technicals for short-term traders. Neither predicts future prices; they tell you what is happening in the markets now and leave you to decide how to play the odds for the future. Neither can be automated any more than dentistry or driving can be automated.

Rating Yourself

Below 31 Poor. Do not despair, you are just starting to test yourself. Go back, reread the recommended literature, and then retake this test.
31–36 Fairly good. You have grasped the basic ideas. Look up the answers to the questions you have missed. Review them and retake this test in a few days.
37–41 Excellent. Armed with this understanding, you are ready to move up and tackle the 3 M's of successful trading.

Required Reading

Elder, Alexander. *Come into My Trading Room* (New York: John Wiley & Sons, 2002). See Part One "Financial Trading for Babes in the Woods."

Additional Reading

Elder, Alexander. *Trading for a Living* (New York: John Wiley & Sons, 1993). See "The Odds Against You" (pages 6–11).

MIND—
THE DISCIPLINED TRADER

Answer 9

C. 2 and 5. Give yourself five points for choosing the correct answer, or two points if you answered B (one correct out of two).

There is only one rational reason to trade—to make money, or to be more exact, to beat riskless rate of return, such as Treasury bills. Trading as an escape from boredom tends to be a very expensive pastime. Discipline and determination are more important than intelligence. As Churchill once said, "It is not the size of the dog in the fight, but the size of the fight in the dog."

Answer 10

A. 4

B. 1, 2

C. 3

Give yourself a point for each correct answer.

Your broker said the stock goes up before a split? Why not get the history of its splits and check for yourself? If you cannot find that history, you have no business trading. The rate of return on an advisor's model portfolio is good for daydreaming but has little connection to how much you will lose taking his advice next year. The Fed announces its meetings well in advance, and you should know that and be ready, reducing your positions if uncertain about the trend. A stock at its two-year low is in a downtrend and may hit a three-year low next; a trend in force is likely to continue.

Answer 11

C. 1, 2, and 3. Give yourself four points for answering C, or two points for any other answer.

Ignorance is the bane of beginners, but a person who keeps losing has to look inward and search for a self-destructive streak. Under-capitalized traders cannot practice sound money management, which is essential for success. Markets are full of bad advice, but it is your responsibility to tell the good from the bad or stand aside if you are not sure.

Answer 12

3. Give yourself three points for choosing the correct answer.

Active alcoholics and losers are in denial, not seeing the depth of their downfall. To help a loser or an alcoholic break through denial is to do him a favor. Overstressed losers often develop physical problems, although not nearly as severe as chronic alcoholics.

Answer 13

1. C

2. B

3. A

4. D

Give yourself a point for each correct answer.

The key difference between a businessman's risk and a loss is the fact that the risk is limited to a small percentage of the account. Both can hurt an account and impact a trader's survival, but a thoughtful businessman limits his risk to contain the damage and promote long-term survival and success.

Answer 14

B. 2 and 5. Give yourself five points for choosing this answer, or two points if you answered C or D (one correct out of two).

The secret of trading is that there is no secret. Success requires hard work, discipline, flair, and attention to detail. It requires your undivided attention, especially in the beginning, while you're still learning the basics. Trading rules are very attractive—you may bet on a race after it starts and exit before it ends. Still, the battle for survival and profit is full of dangers, while its entertainment value distracts most people.

Answer 15

D. 1, 2, 3, and 4. Give yourself five points for answering D, or two points if you answered C or E.

A professional trader stands apart from the crowd and makes his own decisions. When the market throws him a curve, he doesn't blame anyone, but finds out what he should have done differently. He gets an edge from having plans for rallies and declines, allowing him to move ahead and act, while others are just starting to figure out what to do. He is rarely eager to share his knowledge because most people ask for methods, while he knows that the key to winning is discipline, which is hard to teach.

Answer 16

E. All of the above. Give yourself five points for answering correctly.

A disciplined person puts trading first, and works on it daily. He tests every rule, reviews markets for trading signals, and keeps elaborate written records, which allow him to review the behavior of the market, as well as his own, and make the necessary corrections. Discussing open trades with others is one of the most subversive behaviors, which is why a disciplined trader does not do it.

Answer 17

1. C

2. D

3. E

4. B

5. A

Give yourself a point for each correct answer.

Keeping your records up to date is one of the best indicators of your level of discipline. You will benefit from analyzing your records, but the mere fact of starting to keep them and keeping them up to date will put you a step ahead of the crowd.

Answer 18

E.   1 and 4. Give yourself 4 points for answering correctly.

All traders, especially beginners, must focus on a few markets and keep grading their performance. Having too much money and chasing too many stocks tends to lead to sloppy trading. Making money is the overall goal of trading, but learning to trade is the essential first step. It is easier and less stressful to learn while trading a relatively small account. A feeling of excitement is a sign of trouble. The best trades often look iffy at first, and we take them only because our rules force us to do so.

Rating Yourself

Below 33 Poor. Trading psychology is too important a component of trading success to skip over. The psychological demands of trading are quite different from those of the corporate life. Independence, initiative, and personal accountability are among the essential traits of a good trader. You cannot move forward until you get higher grades on this test. Please return to the recommended reading materials, study them, and retake this test a few days later.

33–38 Fairly good. You have grasped the basic ideas, but this is not enough because trading psychology is so important. Look up the answers to the questions you missed. Think about them, review the recommended literature, and retake this test in a few days.

39–44 Excellent, even if you did not get a perfect score. Review those questions on which you did not receive a perfect score to find out whether you made an error or simply exercised an independent approach to psychological tasks.

Required Reading

Elder, Alexander. *Come into My Trading Room* (New York: John Wiley & Sons, 2002). See Chapter 4 "Mind—The Disciplined Trader."

Additional Reading

Douglas, Mark. *The Disciplined Trader* (New York: New York Institute of Finance, 1990).

Elder, Alexander. *Trading for a Living* (New York: John Wiley & Sons, 1993). See "Individual Psychology" and "Mass Psychology" (pages 11–68).

LeFevre, Edwin. *Reminiscences of a Stock Operator* (New York: George H. Doran Company, 1923).

BASIC CHARTING

Answer 19

C. 4 and 5. Give yourself four points for choosing this answer, or two
points if you answered B (one correct out of two).

Prices are not a mirror image of values and can swing considerably
above and below value. Undecided traders who have the money and
watch the market influence it by their presence, putting pressure on
buyers and sellers to act faster.

Answer 20

1. C

2. A

3. B

4. D

Give yourself a point for each correct answer.

Nonprofessional traders are more likely to form their opinions in
the evening and place orders before going to work in the morning.
Professionals are more likely to dominate the market near closing time.
The high tick of every bar shows the limit of bullish power and the lowest tick the limit of bearish power during that bar.

Answer 21

1. C, D

2. B, C

3. A

4. E

5. B

6. D

Give yourself a point for each correct answer (half a point if you got one out of two). Add two points if you got the bonus question right, or a point for getting it partly right.

Uptrendlines connect bottoms of rallies (line A), and downtrendlines connect tops of declines (line B). Zones that served as support on the way down become resistance on the way up, and vice versa (line C). The behavior of prices at the tops sometimes mirrors that at the nearby bottoms—a false upside breakout B was followed by a false downward breakout D. Notice that Figure 3.1 is the chart of the Mexico Index— technical analysis knows no borders.

At the right edge, neutral to bullish. Prices are rallying from a false downside breakout, a bullish pattern. The rally is seven days old and approaching a downtrendline, where prices are likely to run into stiff resistance—potentially bearish. If prices break through, the next upside target will be at the level of the early July peak.

Answer 22

1. D

2. A

3. B, C, E

4. F

Give yourself a point for each correct answer (half a point if you missed a tail). Add two points if you got the bonus question right, or a point for getting it partly right.

Downtrendlines (A) connect successively lower tops of rallies, and uptrendlines (D) track rising bottoms. A break of a trendline often signals the end of a trend. Tails (B, C, and E) show what levels prices have tested and rejected. Prices recoil from kangaroo tails. Channel lines (F) can be drawn parallel to trendlines, framing the limits of bullishness and bearishness.

At the right edge—toppy, time to take profits on long positions. The stock is overbought, hitting its upper channel line—short-term bearish. Wait for a pullback into the lower half of the channel before going long.

Answer 23

1. C-D, G-H

2. A, I, J

3. E

4. F

5. A-B, J-K

Give yourself a point for each correct answer (half a point if you got one but not the other occurrence). Add two points if you got the bonus question right, or a point for getting it partly right.

Price levels that serve as support on the way down become resistance on the way up, which is especially well illustrated by line C-D. Volume spikes A, I, and J indicate that a move is nearing an end. A decline may stop immediately, as it did in area I, or continue to slide, as it did in areas A and J, creating bullish divergences A-B and J-K. Areas E and F are among several examples on this chart in which volume rises during downswings and shrinks on upswings, which is typical bear market behavior.

At the right edge—bullish in the short run, bearish for the longer term. Merck is in a major downtrend, having fallen from above 95 to near 60 in the eight months covered by this chart. Prices are inching higher toward a heavy overhead resistance G-H, while volume is shrinking, showing that bulls are weak and prices are likely to recoil once they reach their overhead resistance.

Rating Yourself

Below 21 Poor. Chart reading is basic literacy for market analysts. Indicators are important, but first you need to get a handle on the basics. Please return to the recommended reading materials, study them, and retake this test a few days later, before proceeding to the rest of the *Study Guide.*

21–25 Fairly good. You understand and can use the key concepts of charting. Still, it would pay to return to the recommended materials, review them, fill in the gaps, and retake the test before proceeding to more advanced computerized analysis.

26–29 Excellent. You can read the charts like an open book. Time to move on and test your knowledge of modern computerized technical analysis.

Required Reading

Elder, Alexander. *Come into My Trading Room* (New York: John Wiley & Sons, 2002). See "Basic Charting" in Chapter 5 (pages 64–80).

Additional Reading

Edwards, Robert D., and John Magee. *Technical Analysis of Stock Trends* (1948) (New York: New York Institute of Finance, 1992).

Elder, Alexander. *Trading for a Living* (New York: John Wiley & Sons, 1993). See "Classical Chart Analysis" (pages 69–114).

Schabacker, Richard W. *Technical Analysis and Stock Market Profits* (1932) (London: Pearson Professional Limited, 1997).

INDICATORS—
FIVE BULLETS TO A CLIP

Answer 24

1. B

2. C

3. D

4. A

Give yourself a point for each correct answer.

Both packages need to be fed fresh data and both can display charts and indicators, but that's where their paths diverge. Toolboxes help analyze the data but leave trading decisions to you. Black boxes claim to liberate you from the onerous task of thinking, as they issue trading commands. Neither guarantees a profit, but at least with a toolbox, if you lose money, you can learn from your mistake instead of scapegoating the software.

Answer 25

1. A

2. B

3. B

4. A

5. B

Give yourself a point for each correct answer.

There are many more oscillators than trend-following indicators. When you trade, it is important to choose a few indicators from each group and combine them in order to balance their messages.

Answer 26

1. B

2. A

3. B

4. B

5. A

Give yourself a point for each correct answer.

The idea is to choose your favorite timeframe and then begin by analyzing the next higher one before returning to your favorite. Longer-term charts help identify bigger trends and make strategic decisions. Two timeframes are enough—you certainly never need more than three—making a weekly chart superfluous for day-traders. Rallies are bigger than declines in bull markets, and this applies to their duration as well as to their extent.

Answer 27

1. D

2. A

3. B

4. E

5. C

Give yourself a point for each correct answer.

The slope of an MA shows whether bulls or bears are in control. The shorter an MA, the more "whippy" it gets. Position traders should average closing prices, but day-traders can average high, low, and close. Exponential moving averages, unlike simple ones, are not distorted by dropping off old data. A moving average shows the average consensus of value, and buying near the MA means buying value.

Answer 28

1. I

2. A, L

3. E, G, H, J

4. D, F, K

5. M

6. B

7. B-C

Give yourself a point for each correct answer (half a point if you missed one of several occurrences). Add two points if you got the bonus question right, or a point for getting it partly right.

Upturns and downturns of a moving average identify trend changes; these are the most important messages of an MA. Buying at a rising EMA (exponential moving average) means buying value, whereas chasing rallies leads to greater fool theory trades—overpaying and hoping that a greater fool will pay even more down the road. The letter L identifies a downtrend. Shorting in area M means shorting value, expecting to cover below value. The kangaroo tail B serves as the first low of a double bottom; prices try to grind down into that area but fail, and a strong rally ensues.

At the right edge—bearish. The trend is down, identified by the EMA, which is pushing lower. The shorting signal M is still in effect. Keep a stop above the previous week's high because if prices rise above it they will complete a minor double bottom, including a false downside breakout, and the EMA will turn up.

Answer 29

1. E

2. A

3. C

4. D

5. B

Give yourself a point for each correct answer.

The upper channel line reflects the normal limits of market optimism, the lower line the normal limits of market pessimism. In uptrends, the envelope hugs rally peaks, while lows may not reach the lower channel line; in downtrends, the lows touch an envelope, while the highs may not reach it. The longer the timeframe, the wider the envelope; the weekly envelope is about twice as wide as the daily in the same market. A well-drawn envelope contains about 95% of recent market data, while Bollinger bands expand and contract with market volatility.

Answer 30

1. C, E, F

2. D, G

3. A, H, I, K

4. B, J

Give yourself a point for each correct answer (half a point if you missed one of several occurrences). Add two points if you got the bonus question right, or a point for getting it partly right.

The time to buy is when the trend is up, identified by a rising moving average. Buying near the rising EMA is a value trade. When prices hit the upper channel line, they show that optimism is rampant, the market is overbought, and it is a good time to sell and take profits. Reverse the procedure in downtrends; when the EMA is down, short near its level and cover when pessimism is overdone, with prices hitting the lower channel line.

At the right edge—bearish to neutral. The trend is down, prices have already touched their EMA, and are headed lower. If, within the next few days, there is a rally above 75, touching the EMA, you may get a chance to sell short and then look to cover near the lower channel line. If not, stand aside and continue to monitor the stock. The downtrend is getting a little long in the tooth, and you should be alert to the flattening of the EMA; when it turns up, it will give a strong buy signal.

Answer 31

1. B (27%)

2. C (14%)

3. D (−25%—loss)

4. A (39%)

Give yourself a point for each correct answer.

Measure the height of a channel from the upper to the lower channel line. If you take 30% of that distance or more out of a trade, it is an A trade; 20% or better earns you a B; 10% or better a C; and anything lower, including a loss, a D. A trade is not complete until you have rated your performance on this scale.

Answer 32

1. D

2. E

3. A

4. C

5. B

Give yourself a point for each correct answer.

MACD-lines is the primary indicator, and MACD-Histogram is derived from it, tracking the distance between the two lines. Divergences between peaks and bottoms of MACD-Histogram and prices are among the strongest signals in technical analysis.

Answer 33

1. F

2. E

3. A-B

4. C-D

5. B

Give yourself a point for each correct answer. Add two points if you got the bonus question right, or a point for getting it partly right.

Prices fall to a new low A, rally, and then fall to a lower low B, where MACD-Histogram traces a more shallow bottom. Notice a slight rally above the centerline between the two lows, "breaking the back of the bear." This strong bullish message is reinforced by a tail in point B. Prices rally to a new high C, pause, and then rise even higher at D, while MACD-Histogram completes a bearish divergence, rising to a very shallow top, with a fall below the centerline between the two peaks. Divergences are the strongest signals of MACD-Histogram, but there are many more ordinary rises and declines, confirming market moves, not only in areas E and F, but all over the chart.

At the right edge—bearish. MACD-Histogram is declining, confirming the downtrend of the EMA.

Answer 34

Phrase 4 does not apply. Give yourself three points for choosing the correct answer.

Force Index measures price change between yesterday and today, but it uses the absolute value of today's volume rather than any change.

Answer 35

1. B, C

2. E, F, G

3. A

4. A, D, E, H

Give yourself a point for each correct answer (half a point if you missed one of several occurrences). Add two points if you got the bonus question right, or a point for getting it partly right.

Force Index gives buy signals when it declines below zero during uptrends. You can find other points, in addition to B and C, where the EMA rises while Force Index becomes negative, giving a buy signal. Force Index gives sell signals when it rises above zero during downtrends. It identified shorting opportunities at points E, F, and G, as well as many others. The bullish divergence in area A develops when prices try to break down to a new low, while the lows of Force Index become more and more shallow. The spikes of Force Index identify exhaustion moves. This chart captures a bearish period in the life of GX, but even so, most downward spikes of Force index lead to substantial rallies or a pause in the downtrend.

At the right edge of the chart—neutral to bearish. The trend is down, the latest spike has interrupted the decline, and prices are likely to hold flat for a while. Watch out for either a breaking of the low H or a bullish divergence to tell you whether the decline is likely to continue or reverse.

Answer 36

1. D

2. E

3. A

4. C

5. B

Give yourself a point for choosing the correct answer.

While the slope of an EMA identifies the trend, Bull Power and Bear Power show how far the high and the low of each bar deviate from the EMA. The time to buy in an uptrend is when a bar straddles the EMA, but Bear Power begins to slip. The time to sell short in a downtrend is when a bar straddles the EMA, but Bull Power begins to weaken.

Answer 37

1. A, C, D

2. F

3. B

4. B-E

5. E

Give yourself a point for each correct answer (half a point if you missed one of several occurrences). Add two points if you got the bonus question right, or a point for getting it partly right.

When the trend, identified by the slope of the EMA, is up and Bear Power becomes negative but then ticks upward, it gives a buy signal. This occurred three times during the uptrend of April–May. The opposite, a shorting signal, occurs when the EMA signals a downtrend, and Bull Power rises to or above zero, but then ticks downward. Whenever Bull Power traces a new record peak for the past several months, it identifies great power of bulls and calls for higher prices ahead. Shortly before entering area E, Bull Power became negative for the first time since the beginning of the rally; when it rose to a new, lower peak and then ticked down, it completed a bearish divergence. That strong sell signal was confirmed by a kangaroo tail; important technical signals often confirm one another.

At the right edge of the chart—bearish. The trend, identified by the EMA, is down, and Bear Power is becoming deeper, while bulls are underwater. Wait for a rally to the EMA to add to shorts.

Answer 38

Choice 4. Give yourself four points if you identified it.

Stochastic is an oscillator whose overbought and oversold readings identify the best areas for buying and selling. Its divergences, as well as those of most other indicators, give the strongest buy and sell signals. One thing that Stochastic, as well as other oscillators, does not do is identify trends; that is the job of trend-following indicators, such as moving averages and MACD.

Answer 39

1. C, E, I, J, L

2. A, B, D, F, G, H, K

3. I-J

4. A-B, G-H

Give yourself a point for each correct answer (half a point if you missed one of several occurrences). Add two points if you got the bonus question right, or a point for getting it partly right.

Stochastic identifies overbought conditions and gives sell signals when it reaches its upper reference line and turns down. It identifies oversold conditions and gives buy signals when it reaches its lower reference line and turns up. Divergences between indicators and prices provide some of the strongest signals in technical analysis. The stock rallies to a higher high at B than at A, but Stochastic turns down from a lower peak, providing an extra powerful sell signal. This pattern recurs in area G-H, just as the stock is knocking its head against the resistance area above 47.50. When different technical patterns flash the same signals, they confirm one another, reinforcing each other's message.

At the right edge of the chart—neutral. The stock has just broken down to a new low, while Stochastic is not confirming. Wait for the indicator to tick up with your finger on the trigger. If it ticks up from a higher level than in area M, it will complete a bullish divergence and give a strong buy signal. On the other hand, if Stochastic does not turn up and create a bullish divergence, it will confirm the strength of the downtrend—stay short.

Rating Yourself

Below 58 Poor. Computerized indicators are powerful tools, offering important insights into crowd behavior. You need to understand them better before moving on to trading. Please return to the recommended reading materials, study them, and retake this test a few days later, before proceeding to the rest of the *Study Guide.*

58–70 Fairly good. You have grasped the key concepts of computerized technical analysis. Now decide whether your current level of understanding is sufficient for your style of trading or whether you should return to the recommended materials, review them, and retake the test before proceeding.

71–86 Excellent. You have a handle on computerized technical analysis. Now that you know how to read the markets, it is time to move on and test your knowledge of trading.

Required Reading

Elder, Alexander. *Come into My Trading Room* (New York: John Wiley & Sons, 2002). See "Indicators—Five Bullets to a Clip" in Chapter 5 (pages 80–117).

Additional Reading

Elder, Alexander. *Trading for a Living* (New York: John Wiley & Sons, 1993). See "Computerized Technical Analysis" (pages 115–166).

LeBeau, Charles, and David W. Lucas. *Technical Traders Guide to Computer Analysis of the Futures Market* (New York: McGraw-Hill, 1991).

Murphy, John J. *Technical Analysis of the Financial Markets* (Englewood Cliffs, NJ: Prentice-Hall, 1999).

TRADING

Answer 40

D. 1, 2, 3, and 4. Give yourself four points for choosing the correct
    answer (two points if you answered C or E, partly correct).

A good trading system pulls out a few key factors from the huge mass
of market information. Market-driving factors keep slowly changing,
which is why system parameters must be tweaked with the passage of
time. Discretionary traders with a good feel for the markets focus their
attention on different factors at different times. All beginners are pre-
occupied with entries, but you get paid for exiting trades. An automatic
system, especially if purchased from a vendor, is a gambler's dream, but
trading requires persistent work.

Answer 41

C. 1, 2, and 3. Give yourself four points for choosing the correct
    answer.

To be worth trading, a system must provide a positive mathematical
expectation of generating more money than it loses over a period of time.
The only way to find out is to test the system yourself. Computerized testing may be more objective, but manual testing more closely replicates the
experience of trading the markets, with all its psychological stresses. You
have to manually test your system to find whether it fits your tempera-
ment as well as your wallet. Most parameters of a trading system can be

tweaked, except for a few inviolate rules, including money management rules. Even if a system seems to do better after dropping those rules, you should not expose your account to unlimited risk.

Answer 42

C. 1, 2, and 3. Give yourself four points for choosing the correct answer.

The main value of paper trading is it allows you to test your discipline and ability to do homework day after day, although most people simply escape into it after losing money. If done right, paper trading takes just as much time as the real thing. The results of paper trading almost always look better than real trading, because there is no emotional pressure from risking money.

Answer 43

1. C

2. D

3. A

4. D

5. B

Give yourself a point for each correct answer.

You cannot argue with the direction or the numerical value of an indicator, which is why their signals are more objective than chart patterns. The three indicator groups almost always give contradictory signals. One of the main challenges in technical analysis is to reconcile those conflicts and profit from them.

Answer 44

D. 1, 2, 3, and 4. Give yourself four points for choosing the correct answer.

The contradictions between signals in different timeframes present a challenge, as well as an opportunity. We can filter them against one another, leaving only the best signals. Long-term as well as short-term charts are defined by their relationships to the intermediate timeframe, using the Rule of Five. Short-term charts allow you to get closer to the markets, but it is much more important to begin your analysis by making a strategic decision on long-term charts.

Answer 45

Phrase 3 is correct. Give yourself four points for choosing the right answer.

One of the key rules of the Triple Screen is to make your decisions in several timeframes, moving down from the longest to the shortest. If you work with weekly, daily, and intraday charts, then make your strategic decision, either bullish or bearish, on the weekly chart, then tactical on the dailies, and find entry and exit points using intraday charts.

Answer 46

Choice 4 is not acceptable. Give yourself three points for choosing the right answer.

Buying an upside breakout puts you in the direction of the trend, whereas buying pullbacks provides less expensive entries. These are all acceptable methods, but it is seldom a good idea to put in orders without even knowing what price you will have to pay at the opening tomorrow.

Answer 47

D. 1, 2, 3, and 4. Give yourself four points for choosing the right answer.

There are many methods for exiting trades. A longer-term trader will watch the EMA, the resistance, or the channel, whereas the shorter-term trader will focus on the channel or the spikes in Force Index. Use the method that appeals to you, but do not make your decisions "on the gut." If you sell on the gut today, you will be tempted to buy on the gut tomorrow, and that's where the real trouble will start.

Rating Yourself

Below 24 Poor. You need to give yourself a little more time to learn about trading before putting money on the line. Testing systems and indicators, while combining different timeframes, is a key concept of successful trading. Please return to the recommended reading materials, study them, and retake this test a few days later before proceeding to the rest of the *Study Guide.*

24–28 Fairly good. You understand the key concepts of trading. Still, it would make sense to read up on the questions that you have missed. This topic is too important to leave out a few blanks.

29–32 Excellent. You understand the key trading ideas. If you are interested in day-trading, please proceed to the next chapter; otherwise, skip it and go directly to Advanced Concepts, Chapter 7.

Required Reading

Elder, Alexander. *Come into My Trading Room* (New York: John Wiley & Sons, 2002). See "System Testing" and "Triple Screen Update" in Chapter 6 (pages 121–134).

Additional Reading

Elder, Alexander. *Trading for a Living* (New York: John Wiley & Sons, 1993). See "Triple Screen Trading System" (pages 235–243).

Kaufman, Perry J. *Smarter Trading* (New York: McGraw-Hill, 1995).

Schwager, Jack D. *Technical Analysis of the Futures Markets* (New York: John Wiley & Sons, 1995).

DAY-TRADING

Answer 48

D. 1, 2, 3, and 4. Give yourself four points for choosing the right answer.

In day-trading, profits are smaller and expenses are higher. There are long periods of "dead time," but when a signal comes, you must recognize it instantly and trade without pausing to ruminate. Losses are generally smaller than in position trading because losing trades are closed out no later than at the end of the day.

Answer 49

C. 1 and 4. Give yourself four points for choosing the right answer.

Day-trading demands a much higher degree of concentration than position trading because it does not leave you time to think. Impulsivity is deadly because you have no time to correct your mistakes. Day-trading is an expensive proposition that generates high commissions and leads to purchases of software, data, and other tools, that are the main reasons why brokers and vendors love it. To succeed, you must face your impulsivity and work to reduce it. A written trading plan is a useful step in that direction.

Answer 50

2. Penny stocks are unsuitable for day-trading. Give yourself four points for choosing the right answer.

The two essential criteria for choosing day-trading stocks are liquidity and volatility. You can find stocks that keep making big moves on high volume among the most actives or the most popular stocks. Penny stocks may be promising for investors, but are not good for day-traders because of their narrow intraday ranges and low liquidity.

Answer 51

1. D

2. E

3. C

4. B

5. A

Give yourself a point for each correct answer.

The intraday volume curve is normally U-shaped—highest during the first and last half-hours of trading. Early in the session outsiders crowd into the market, and by the end of the day the pros dominate the action. A wide opening range may define the high and the low of the day, but prices are likely to break out of a narrow opening range.

Answer 52

1. B

2. A

3. D, E, F, G

4. C

5. C-H

Give yourself a point for each correct answer (half a point if you missed one of several occurrences). Add two points if you got the bonus question right, or a point for getting it partly right.

When a downward gap first appears, it is hard to tell whether it is a continuation of the downtrend or an exhaustion move prior to an upside reversal. The downside breakout from the opening range confirms the downtrend and gives the first good shorting signal of the day. The deepening bottoms of MACD-Histogram show that the bears are growing stronger and lead one to expect lower prices ahead. Rallies to the EMA create shorting opportunities throughout the day. During the last hour of trading prices dip to a new low, while MACD-Histogram traces a higher bottom. This bullish divergence gives a buy signal—time to take profits on shorts.

At the right edge of the chart—bearish. The trend is down, and prices closed near the lows; expect a lower opening tomorrow. The beauty of day-trading is that there is no overnight risk. We can wait for the opening, monitor the opening range, and then trade the breakout.

Answer 53

C. 1, 2, and 3. Give yourself four points for choosing the right answer.

The best time to make strategic decisions is before the opening—if the stock does this, I will trade this way, and so on. Then, as you review your stocks throughout the day, you are ready to act fast whenever your conditions are met. There is no harm listening to tips, as long as you put them through the same screens as your regular stocks; perhaps they should be added to the regular list. Trading in a room full of people is much more likely to lead to emotional decisions. Successful traders almost always sit at the edge of the trading room, isolating themselves from the masses.

Rating Yourself

Below 21 Poor. With grades like this, you should steer clear of day-trading. If you are intent on day-trading, please return to the recommended materials and study them carefully before retaking this test.

21–24 Fairly good. You understand the key concepts of day-trading. Do yourself a favor, and review the questions that you missed. This topic is too important to leave out a few blanks!

25–28 Excellent. You have a good grasp of the essential concepts. Just keep in mind that the Advanced Concepts, described in the next chapter, also can be applied to day-trading.

Required Reading

Elder, Alexander. *Come into My Trading Room* (New York: John Wiley & Sons, 2002). See "Day-Trading" in Chapter 6 (pages 134–153).

Additional Materials

Appel, Gerald. *Day-Trading with Gerald Appel* (video) (New York: Financial Trading, Inc., 1989).

ADVANCED CONCEPTS

Answer 54

1. E

2. B

3. D

4. F

5. A

6. C

Give yourself a point for each correct answer.

The slope of the EMA reflects the direction of market inertia, whereas the slope of MACD-Histogram shows the direction of market momentum. Combining the messages of these two indicators is the key principle of the Impulse System. The longer you wait to recognize a splash of momentum, the lower the profitability. Taking profits and jumping out of successful trades is the hardest psychological factor of momentum trading.

Answer 55

1. D, F

2. A, B, C, E, G, H

Give yourself a point for each correctly identified cluster. Add two points if you got the bonus question right, or a point for getting it partly right.

Buy signals emerge when both the EMA and MACD-Histogram are rising together; sell signals emerge when both are falling. The weekly uptrend (not shown) gives extra weight to bullish signals. Bearish clusters show reactions against the uptrend, but once those signals cease, the uptrend embarks on its sharpest upmoves.

At the right edge of the chart—neutral. The trend is getting old, and MACD-Histogram is weakening. Tighten stops on long positions.

Answer 56

1. E

2. B, C, F, G

3. A

4. C

5. B, D

6. D-G

Give yourself a point for each correct answer (half a point if you missed one of several occurrences). Add two points if you got the bonus question right, or a point for getting it partly right.

The day begins with a string of shorting signals: a downward gap, followed by a cluster of Impulse sell signals, followed by a downside breakout from the opening range, and then more Impulse sell signals. The deepening bottoms of MACD-Histogram call for lower prices ahead. The best day-trading opportunities tend to present themselves in the beginning of the session, although the Impulse System continues to give sell signals throughout the day. At point G prices sink to a new low, but MACD-Histogram completes a bullish divergence—the last call to take profits on intraday shorts.

At the right edge of the chart—neutral. The trend is down and prices are weak and closing near the lows, but there is a bullish divergence. Tomorrow check the 25-minute chart and be ready to follow the first cluster of the Impulse System signals.

Answer 57

B. 1 and 2. Give yourself four points for choosing the right answer.

Most people are more objective when they do not have money at risk. Before he enters a trade, a rational trader estimates his profit as well as his risk, compares them and makes his go–no go decision. He tries to select trades in which he stands to win more than he risks—the higher the ratio, the better. If the exit target is at a channel line, that target will move with the passage of time, but it is important to have a general idea where it is before you enter.

Answer 58

C. 1, 2, and 3. Give yourself four points for choosing the right answer.

One of the few statistically proven market behaviors is the tendency of prices to fluctuate above and below value. Channels help identify manic levels for selling longs and going short and depressed levels for covering shorts and going long. Before putting on a trade, make sure that the channel is wide enough to be worth trading. A well-drawn channel contains about 95% of prices, but no channel is perfect. Some price swings are so strong that they punch out of the channel, whereas others are too weak to reach it.

Answer 59

1. A, C, D

2. B, E

Give yourself a point for each correctly identified signal. Add two points if you got the bonus question right, or a point for getting it partly right.

   When prices hit the upper line of a well-drawn channel, they reveal market mania and give a sell signal. You can place your sell order in advance, at the channel line. If you are in front of the screen during the day, you may wait for prices to punch above that line and then exit when prices fail to make a new high for the day or, as a fallback, when they weaken and hit the channel wall from above. The time to cover shorts is when prices hit the lower channel wall. Notice a beautiful buy signal between points C and D. Prices came back to touch the EMA before embarking on their most dynamic rally. The only way to have caught that buy signal was to estimate tomorrow's EMA value each day and place a buy order there for the day ahead.

   At the right edge of the chart—bullish. The EMA has ticked up, and prices straddle the EMA, offering a value trade. It is time to buy and be ready to take profits near the upper channel line.

Answer 60

True   1, 4, 5

False   2, 3

Give yourself a point for each correct answer.

   Stops must be defined by both technical analysis and money management and placed immediately after entering a trade. Most traders should place actual stop orders: only the pros of proven discipline may use mental stops. Relying on so-called advanced analysis instead of stops is a sign of arrogance that has been the undoing of countless traders.

Answer 61

1. B

2. E

3. D

4. C

5. A

6. F

Give yourself a point for each correct answer.

Market noise is the extent by which today's extreme price extends outside yesterday's extreme—the high in downtrends, the low in uptrends. Average Penetration is the average level of market noise during the lookback period. We multiply Average Upside Penetration by the coefficient and add it to the highs to place stops in downtrends, or multiply Average Downside Penetration by the coefficient and subtract it from the lows to place stops in uptrends.

Answer 62

D. 1, 2, 3, and 4. Give yourself four points for choosing the right answer.

Margin works great when you're right, but hits you even harder on losing trades. It raises the cost of trading, as well as the stress level, because with margin you trade beyond your means. A small trader who goes on margin can make more money when he is right, but is almost certain to underperform a cash trader in the long run.

Answer 63

1. A

2. C

3. A

4. B

5. B

Give yourself a point for each correct answer.

Trends tend to emerge from sleepy trading ranges in formerly obscure stocks. The width of a channel matters little if you are positioning yourself for a major trend. Stocks are likely to swing within the trend, requiring wider stops. Wide channels, active trading, and taking profits at the channel line are required for swing trading. Anyone who says that trading, either trends or channels, is easy is either a genius or, more likely, a beginner.

Answer 64

Item 3 is not a factor. Give yourself four points for choosing the right answer.

The more time to expiration, the closer the exercise price, the higher the volatility and the interest rates, and the more expensive an option. Options are remarkably blind to trends, even though they are highly attuned to market volatility.

Answer 65

1. B

2. E

3. A

4. C

5. D

Give yourself a point for each correct answer.

Options offer an enormous range of choices, from buying calls out-right—the beginners' favorite tactic—all the way up to diagonal butter-fly spreads and beyond. Sophisticated traders tend to write rather than buy options.

Answer 66

C. 1, 2, and 3. Give yourself four points for choosing the right answer.

Writing covered options is an expensive proposition because of com-missions on both stocks and options; naked writing exposes traders to unlimited risk. For those reasons, money management is the corner-stone of any intelligent option-writing campaign. Option writers profit from selling hope—it is better to sell hope that is unlikely to be fulfilled, writing calls in downtrends and puts in uptrends. Time works for the writer because the options he sells lose value with each passing day. There is no reason to wait for the expiration if the option you sold has lost almost all its value—buy it back, kill the risk, and move on to the next trade.

Answer 67

1. D

2. E

3. A

4. B

5. C

Give yourself a point for each correct answer.

If you grow wheat and hedge by selling a corresponding quantity of futures contracts, you eliminate price risk between that time and the har-vest, when wheat is sold to consumers and futures bought back. Razor-thin margins in futures lure beginners into overtrading, and they take on more risk than they can handle. Faraway months normally sell for more than nearby ones because of storage and insurance costs; an inverted market, with more expensive nearby contracts, reflects very high demand, which is bullish. Industrial producers and consumers can legally trade futures using inside information. Supply-driven markets tend to be fast and furious; bad weather can stress the balance between supply and demand much faster that changing consumer tastes.

Rating Yourself

Below 56 Poor. If you have already learned conventional methods, you should be able to do better with these advanced techniques. Please return to the recommended materials, study them, and retake this test a few days later.

56–66 Fairly good. You are starting to get a handle on new, unconventional methods. It would be a good idea to return to the recommended literature, review answers to the questions you missed, then return to the *Study Guide* a few days later.

67–77 Excellent. You are way ahead of the game. Now tighten your seat belt because you will be moving forward to the topic that separates the winners from the losers—money management.

Recommended Reading

Elder, Alexander. *Come into My Trading Room* (New York: John Wiley & Sons, 2002). See Chapter 5 "Trading."

Additional Reading

McMillan, Lawrence G. *Options as a Strategic Investment,* 3rd ed. (New York: New York Institute of Finance, 1999).

Teweles, Richard J., and Frank J. Jones. *The Futures Game,* 3rd ed. (New York: McGraw-Hill, 1998).

MONEY MANAGEMENT

Answer 68

Choice 5 is correct. Give yourself four points for choosing the right answer.

A system with a positive expectation allows you to make money over a long series of trades—it gives you an edge but not a guarantee of success. A system may deliver more losing than winning trades but still be profitable if winners are bigger than losers. Each individual trade is dicey, but a well-designed system creates a positive expectation over a long series of trades. Money management can protect a trader using such a system, but it cannot turn a losing system into a winner.

Answer 69

1. 533

2. 24

3. 69

4. 18,750

5. 37.5%

Give yourself a point for each correct answer.

Modern society makes it easy to live without counting, but if you want to succeed in trading you have to think—and count—on your feet. You may own a calculator, but you must be able at least to estimate the results of any arithmetic operation in your head.

Answer 70

Choice 3 is correct. Give yourself four points for choosing the right answer.

The 2% Rule, the most important rule of money management, protects you from ever losing more than 2% of your account equity on any single trade. If your stop is close and risk per share is small, you may trade a bigger size, as long as you are mindful of the overnight risk. If the stop is far and risk per share is high, the size has to be smaller because your total dollar risk may never exceed 2% of your account equity.

Answer 71

B. 1 and 2. Give yourself four points for choosing the right answer, or two points if you answered C.

According to the 2% Rule, you may not risk more than 2% of your account equity on any given trade, including commissions and slippage. Having a $50,000 account allows you to risk no more than $1,000 per trade. Trade 1: you risk $1.50 per share on 500 shares, for a total of $750, which is acceptable. Trade 2: you risk $3 per share on 300 shares, for a total of $900, which is acceptable. Both trades leave room for slippage and commissions. Trade 3: you risk $1 per share on 1,000 shares, for a total of $1,000, which leaves no room for slippage or commissions. Trade 4: you risk $6 per share on 200 shares, for a total of $1,200, which would break the 2% limit. Trade 5: you risk $2 per share on 700 shares, for a total of $1,400, which would break the 2% limit.

Answer 72

A. 1, 3

B. 2, 4, 5

Give yourself a point for each correct answer.

The key rule of money management is never risk more than 2% of your account on any given trade. The dividing line is drawn at 2%—if you risk less, it is a businessman's risk, and if you risk more, you are staring at a loss. Two percent of $100,000 comes to $2,000, 2% of $20,000 to only $400—this is your maximum permitted risk per trade. Trade 1: you risk $1.25 per share on 1,000 shares for a total of $1,250— less than 2% of a $100,000 account (businessman's risk). Trade 2: you risk $2 per share on 300 shares for a total of $600—more than 2% of a $20,000 account (risk of loss). Trade 3: you risk $1.50 per share on 200 shares for a total of $300—less than 2% of a $20,000 account (businessman's risk). Trade 4: you risk $4 per share on 1,000 shares for a total of $4,000—more than 2% of a $100,000 account (risk of loss). Trades 2 and 4 could still be done, only with a smaller size, pushing the risk below 2% of each account. In trade 5, without a stop, what if that stock slides to $5, which could happen in a bear market? Busting through the 2% risk limit can damage even the biggest account.

Answer 73

Yes. Give yourself three points for choosing the right answer.

Bill plans to risk $4 per share on 100 shares, or $400, plus commissions and slippage. The 2% Rule allows him to risk up to $500. His trade is within the limits of the 2% Rule. Still, he is pushing it a bit. As a beginner, he'd better stay farther away from the 2% limit. Perhaps he could focus on lower-priced stocks and work on his analysis, entry, and exit techniques without coming so close to the 2% limit.

Answer 74

Yes. Give yourself three points for choosing the right answer.

Since a gold futures contract has 100 ounces, a trader wins or loses $100 whenever gold rises or falls $1 per ounce. Gary plans to risk $300, plus commission and slippage. The 2% Rule allows him to risk a maximum of $400. The 2% Rule allows him to take that trade. Gary is aiming for a $900 profit, risking $300. Those are good odds, but his plan illustrates how hard it is to trade a small account. A mere $3 move against him puts him near the limit of his risk tolerance. He may want to look into trading smaller minicontracts.

Answer 75

No. Give yourself three points for choosing the right answer.

The 2% Rule limits Susan's maximum allowed risk to $1,000. Risking $2.50 per share on 500 shares would expose $1,250 to risk, plus commissions and slippage. This trade would violate the 2% Rule. Susan has to reduce the number of shares she'll buy. If a proven system gives her this trade, she should take it, but on a smaller scale—300 shares rather than 500.

Answer 76

Choice 3 is correct. Give yourself four points for choosing the right answer.

All of the choices given are helpful, but none compares in importance with having a boss whose main tasks are money management and discipline. People who trade well for institutions can rarely match their performance level once they leave to trade for themselves, because they leave the manager behind. A private trader has to be his own manager, which is why it is essential to write down your trading plans and rate yourself on your adherence to them.

Answer 77

Choice 2 is correct. Give yourself four points for choosing the right answer.

Record your account size at the beginning of the month. To observe the 6% Rule, you must stop trading as soon as your equity dips 6% below that level. Stay out for the balance of the month. Your risk is at its highest when you put on a trade; the total account risk will never exceed 6% because then you simply may not put on another trade. Following the 2% Rule, you may have more than three open positions, if each risks less than 2%.

Answer 78

Yes. Give yourself four points for choosing the right answer.

Six precent of a $90,000 account comes to $5,400—this is Ann's permitted risk of loss for the month. She already lost a total of $2,400 on trades A and B, but trades C and D are moving in her favor, stops are at breakeven, and she has no money at risk in them. This leaves her with $3,000 of permitted risk capital. Trade E would expose $1,500 to risk—this is less than 2% of her account, while her total risk for the month remains below 6%.

Answer 79

No. Give yourself four points for choosing the right answer.

Six percent of a $150,000 account comes to $9,000—this is Peter's permitted risk of loss for the month. No matter how profitable early in the month, he has already lost $5,000 of his starting equity and has two open trades, risking $1,900 and $1,700, for a total of $8,600 either lost or at risk. There is simply no room for one more trade, unless he wants to close out one of the trades in which he has money at risk and free up enough risk capital for a new trade.

Answer 80

Yes. Give yourself four points for choosing the right answer.

Six percent of a $30,000 account comes to $1,800—this is Jim's permitted risk of loss for the month. So far he lost $500, besides having two profitable trades. If he trades the same size in D and E and uses similar stops as in his previous trades, his total risk exposure will be $1,500—below his monthly limit.

Answer 81

True 1, 3, 5

False 2, 4

Give yourself a point for each correct answer.

The less money you risk on any given trade, the more objective you are likely to be, and the more likely that trade is to be a winner. It is important to trade a fairly consistent size and reduce it when losing.

Putting on bigger trades in an attempt to recoup losses is typical amateur behavior. Professionals plan their trades for safety and survival first,
for big profits second. The best trades tend to have very tight stops,
allowing you to trade a large size with a fairly small amount at risk.

Answer 82

Choice 2 is correct. Give yourself four points for choosing the right answer.

Overtrading means risking too much for your account. Making three
trades a day can be a legitimate level of activity for a day-trader, and an
active swing trader may make 10 trades a week when the market is running. The maximum risk per trade in a $100,000 account is $2,000, and
someone who buys right above support with a very tight stop may be
able to afford to trade a big size. The maximum risk for a $100,000
account is $6,000 per month, allowing five open trades risking $1,000
each. Having 10 open positions, whose risk amounts to $7,500, busts
through the 6% Rule and indicates overtrading.

Rating Yourself

Below 54 Poor. Failing this test gives you plenty of company. Most people do not know enough about money management. You must bring
yourself up to speed—this aspect of trading cannot be skipped!
Please return to the recommended materials, study them, and retake
this test a few days later.

54–60 Excellent. You show a level of understanding of trading that few
people possess. If you implement your knowledge in practice, you
should get ahead of the game. Now please move on to the next
essential topics—record keeping and accountability.

Required Reading

Elder, Alexander. *Come into My Trading Room* (New York: John Wiley & Sons,
2002). See Chapter 7 "Money Management Formulas."

Additional Reading

Vince, Ralph. *Portfolio Management Formulas* (New York: John Wiley & Sons,
1990).

THE ORGANIZED TRADER

Answer 83

Factor 3 is correct. Give yourself three points for choosing the right answer.

All factors listed here are important, but none more so than discipline. Markets are full of intelligent people with experience and imagination who have been trained and still fail to make money. Discipline is the key factor; without it all others are useless.

Answer 84

Choice 2. Give yourself four points for choosing the right answer.

Good records are the key factor in disciplined trading. Keeping them leads to a reduction in trading mistakes. No matter how good your records, no matter how proficient you become in trading, nothing permits you to relax your money management discipline; if anything, as traders get better, they tend to tighten their money management.

Answer 85

E. All of the above. Give yourself four points for choosing the right answer.

Entry and exit dates and price levels are the basic starting points for this spreadsheet. It also helps to keep an eye on expenses. A more sophisticated trader uses his spreadsheet to calculate his performance grade for every trade, that is, the percentage of a trading channel caught in that trade. He can also rate the quality of entries and exits—whether he bought or sold closer to the top or the bottom of the daily bar.

Answer 86

C. 1, 2, and 3. Give yourself four points for choosing the right answer.

If you intend to treat trading as a business, you must know its cash position at any given time. Equity in a trading account consists of the current value of all open positions, marking open profits and losses to market, as well as cash and cash equivalents, such as T-bills. Funds outside of your trading account, such as savings or credit lines, are immaterial to your equity.

Answer 87

Trader 5 has the best equity curve. Give yourself four points for choosing the right answer.

Trader 4 earned the biggest profit, but his drawdown is outright scary. A $28,000 drawdown represents more than a quarter of this trader's starting equity. What if such a deep drawdown comes at the very beginning of a money management period? No matter how brilliant a comeback, this kind of trading is an invitation to disaster. Most fund managers look for steady gains with small drawdowns. If your drawdown never goes into double digits, your performance is brilliant.

Answer 88

Choice 4 is correct. Give yourself three points for choosing the right answer.

One chart per entry or exit may not be enough, because entries and exits tend to be complex affairs with several parameters. You may want to print out a weekly, a daily and an intraday chart for an entry and a daily, and an intraday for an exit. Five charts per entry or exit is too much; trading decisions are best reduced to a small number of key parameters.

Answer 89

C. 1, 2, and 3. Give yourself four points for choosing the right answer (two points if you chose D).

Gloating after taking a profit or cringing after taking a loss does nothing to improve future performance. What did I do right? Have I made a mistake? What should I do differently next time? A focused, disciplined trader keeps asking himself these and other questions, and a trading diary helps him answer them. People who have the discipline to keep good records have the discipline to win consistently. Still, it may be impractical for a very active trader to keep a diary of every single trade. In that case, it is important to keep a diary for every second, third, or fifth trade, in strict order, rather than deciding to keep it for "interesting" trades and omitting it for "ordinary" trades. Knowing which is which tends to come well after a trade has been closed out.

Answer 90

Entry—4. 75%.

Exit— 2. 25%.

Give yourself two points for each correct answer.

The entry grade rates the quality of your entry by expressing it as a percentage of that day's range. If the high of the day was 48, the low 44, and you bought at 47, then your entry grade is 75, meaning you missed 75% of the day's range. The lower the percentage while buying, the better. The exit grade rates the quality of your exit. If the high of the day was 54, the low 50, and you sold at 51, your exit grade is 25. It means you captured 25% of that day's range. The higher the percentage, the better for the seller. The idea is to get your buying grade below 50% and your selling grade above 50%. This is much harder to accomplish than it looks.

Answer 91

C. 1, 2, and 3. Give yourself four points for choosing the right answer (two points if you chose B).

Rapidly changing prices affect people like the noise and flashing of slot machines, tempting them to put in another quarter. Making decisions to buy, sell, or stand aside when the markets are closed offers traders the luxury of time. Comparing your stock or future to others adds an extra dimension to your decision-making process. It is a bad idea to ask for advice on specific trades before taking them—those trades are yours and the decision is yours alone.

Answer 92

1. A

2. B

3. C

4. E

5. D

Give yourself a point for each correct answer.

Having to describe a chart forces you to focus on specific signals that led to a trading decision. Live charts often seduce traders into joining emotional crowds; reading your orders from a printed sheet reinforces discipline. If you planned to buy a stock if it trades flat, but it gaps up the next morning and you have not planned for it, there is no reason to trade. When a stock does something you have not anticipated, that is a clear signal that your decision making was not in gear with the market, and putting on a trade is not a good idea.

Answer 93

D. 1, 2, 3, and 4. Give yourself four points for choosing the right answer.

The trader's spreadsheet provides a basic record of every trade, including its performance grade. The equity curve tracks the health of your account as a whole. The trading diary allows you to learn from visual records of past trades. The action plan helps you face the next trading day in a calm and disciplined manner. All of these records are essential for success; only the ABC rating system is optional. You need it if you track a large number of stocks and futures, but can do without it if you watch just a handful.

Answer 94

B. 1 and 2. Give yourself four points for choosing the right answer.

Second-guessing a system, or making trading decisions on the basis of factors which are not included in the system, dramatically increases the range of options but reduces the likelihood of success. Second-guessing raises the level of psychological stress, subverts discipline, and leads to impulsive trading.

Answer 95

C. 1, 2, and 3. Give yourself four points for choosing the right answer.

Telling people about your open positions is like inviting them to watch you get intimate with your significant other. It will make you more popular and invite friendly advice on positions you haven't considered, none of which is likely to lead to a successful outcome. You need to be strong enough to shoulder all the responsibility for a trade; you may discuss it with others only after closing it.

Answer 96

E. All of the above. Give yourself four points for choosing the right answer.

Trading requires time just as much as it requires capital. You need to review all markets in which you are interested at least once a week, usually on weekends. All open positions have to be reviewed daily. You need to keep a timetable of all important news that may impact your market in order to decide whether to hold your position, reduce its size, or get out. Breakouts from opening ranges can help with entries; weak prices near the close can give the signal to get out of a trade. The more time you put into the markets, the more profit they are likely to return to you.

Answer 97

1. A

2. E

3. C

4. D

5. B

Give yourself a point for each correct answer.

The ABC rating system helps traders use their time more efficiently. It calls for a weekly review of all markets you track and sorting them into three groups. A is the most promising, and usually the smallest, group, where you anticipate a trade the next day. Stocks or futures in group A must be reviewed in depth daily. B is the group where you expect a trade within a few days, and its stocks or futures should be reviewed a few days later. C is the group where you do not anticipate a trade for a week, and its stocks or futures can be set aside for the rest of the week.

Answer 98

Combination 4 is correct. Give yourself four points for choosing the right answer.

Strict money management rules are the keystone of any trading plan; they allow you to survive and succeed in the long run. A systems trader must be absolutely strict about his analytic rules, but a discretionary trader has some degree of flexibility. As long as he analyzes multiple timeframes and does not trade against his rules, he has some latitude in choosing his indicators and methods.

Answer 99

Choice 2 is correct. Give yourself four points for choosing the right answer.

Beginners are attracted by tales of huge profits, but professionals focus on survival first. This is why any good trading plan is built on the basis of money management rules. The next goal is to grind out steady profits. Once that goal is being consistently achieved, we can spend more time looking for extraordinary opportunities. Then, if our analysis is right and the market cooperates, we sometimes achieve extraordinary returns.

Answer 100

Sequence 5 is correct. Give yourself four points for choosing the right answer.

Serious trading begins with good records. They come first because they allow you to learn from mistakes as well successes, while you experiment with different techniques. Setting money management rules and recording your compliance with them is the next most important step. The third stage is the development of a decision-making tree.

Rating Yourself

Below 60 Poor. If you failed this test, please go back to the main book, reread the appropriate chapters, and retake this test. The topic is so new and so neglected in trading literature that most people are completely unfamiliar with it. If you master it, you will get far ahead of the crowd. Return to the recommended chapters, study them, and retake this test a few days later.

60–72 Excellent. Your understanding of trading records is uncommon! All that is left now is to set up your own records—and to trade successfully!

Required Reading

Elder, Alexander. *Come into My Trading Room* (New York: John Wiley & Sons, 2002). See Chapter 8 "The Organized Trader" and Chapter 9 "Trading for a Living."

LET'S TRADE:
CASE STUDIES
AND QUESTIONS

LET'S TRADE

The longer you trade, the more you learn—practice will make you a better trader. Be sure to put on many small trades and carefully document every entry and exit. Good records allow you to learn from experience. Trading small will help you keep emotions in check. You will have plenty of time to increase your trading size once you become a competent trader.

Remember this paragraph from *Come Into My Trading Room*:

> Keeping good records is the single most important contribution to your success. If you scrupulously maintain records, review them, and learn from them, your performance will improve. If, at the same time, your money management is in place to ensure survival during the learning process, you're sure to become a success.

This chapter of the *Study Guide* offers you an opportunity to practice making trading decisions and keeping records. Look at the charts in this chapter as if you saw them in your trader's diary. Mark up chart patterns and indicator signals, and write down your comments on the most important points. Make your trading decision and then turn to the Answers chapter to compare your notes with mine and grade your performance.

There are many ways to reach a trading decision. Some serious traders use fundamental analysis, others technical, some combine both, while gamblers trade "from the gut." I like to be aware of the key fundamentals, but my favorite method is technical analysis. Price, time, and volume reflect actions of all market participants—smart and dumb, disciplined and gamblers, rich and poor, long-term and short-term oriented. Prices and indicators are the footprints of bulls and bears. Let us practice reading those footprints in order to find our way.

The charts in this section were printed in December 2001, not long after the disaster of September 11th in New York. In stressful times like these, when fundamentals shift rapidly, technical analysis really shines.

How to Work with These Case Studies

You will see three charts for each trade—two for the entry and one for the exit. For the entry, you will have a weekly and a daily chart. The weekly chart will show about a year and a half of history, a 26-week EMA (solid), a 13-week EMA (dotted), and MACD-Histogram. The daily chart, ending on the same day, will show several months of history, the 22-day and the 13-day EMAs (solid and dotted), a 2-day Force Index, and MACD-Histogram. For exit and reentry decisions, you will see an updated daily chart that will, in addition to the above, show a trading channel centered around the long EMA.

These charts feature some of my favorite indicators, although many others could be used. It would impossible to show all important indicators in a study guide, especially since serious traders always change their sets of technical tools. My main goal here is to demonstrate the need for using multiple timeframes—making a strategic decision on the weekly chart and tactical choices on the daily chart. I also want to illustrate the need for combining several indicators—trend-following and oscillators—to evaluate different aspects of market behavior and make rational trading decisions.

It is your job to find, mark, and document at least two important trading signals on each chart. You will receive a point for each correctly marked signal and bonus points for identifying additional trading signals. Be sure to document each step that you take.

There are eight sets of charts, covering eight trades. Begin by working through an entry in one market, and then grade your performance on that entry. Afterward, work through an exit and grade your performance again, using rating scales in the Answers section. If you are satisfied with your performance, move on to the next trade and repeat this process. If you find that you have done poorly in a trade, return to *Come*

Into My Trading Room and reread the relevant chapters before going any further. This process will put you miles ahead of amateurs and gamblers who jump into the market with both feet, chasing a quick buck— and get taken out feet first. Education, record keeping, and caution are essential for your long-term success, which is the only success worth having in the financial markets.

Please do not try to complete all eight exercises in a single day. Give yourself enough time to think, reflect, reread relevant chapters, and review other charts on your screen. You can take more than a week to work through these exercises.

Here is the recommended sequence of steps as you move through eight trades:

1. Look at the Entry Question page, which shows two unmarked charts—weekly and a daily.

2. Mark two or more trading messages on each chart; make an entry decision and document it.

3. Go to the Entry Answer page for that trade and grade your entry performance. If the grade is satisfactory (above the pass point), proceed as directed below; otherwise, return to *Come Into My Trading Room* and study the relevant chapters.

4. Go to the Exit Question page, which shows an updated unmarked daily chart. Quickly cover it with a sheet of paper.

5. Gently move the sheet from left to right, until you uncover the vertical arrow marking the entry into the trade; from that day onward, move the sheet to the right very slowly, one day at a time, stopping after you uncover each day.

6. Whenever you see an exit point, based on chart or indicator signals, mark it; whenever you see a likely reentry point, mark it also. Most charts have more than one exit and reentry point.

7. Once you reach the right edge of the chart, go to the Exit Answer page and rate your performance. If the grade is satisfactory (above the pass point), proceed as directed below; otherwise, return to *Come Into My Trading Room* and study the relevant chapters.

8. Proceed to the next trade and repeat the process.

Technical analysis is partly a science and partly an art—partly objective and partly subjective. There are two main approaches to using it in trading—systematic and discretionary. Systematic traders test and automate every step. Discretionary traders change their tools as markets evolve. If you are a systematic trader, you will test all the tools and apply them in an absolutely uniform manner. As a discretionary trader, I adjust my tools and every once in a while try to anticipate indicator signals. The trick is to anticipate them ever so slightly, without going too far out on a limb, and use the protection of money management.

Intelligent traders may disagree about trading signals. This is why a professional trader is unlikely to get a perfect score on these tests. He will bring his personality into the picture and interpret markets slightly differently. Show me an experienced trader with independent judgment, good records, and solid money management, and I will show you a winner. What if you see some charts in a different light than I do? I fear an avalanche of e-mails with questions, and not enough hours in the day to answer all. The only place where we can butt heads and argue about trades late into the night is in Traders' Camps. Bring in your differences, and we will resolve them. Just be sure to keep good records of your decisions. Now, let's go look for trades!

Trade 1: Oracle Corp ORCL—*Entry Question*

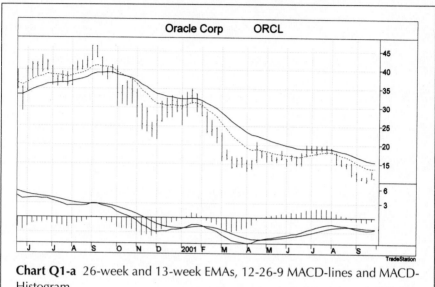

Chart Q1-a 26-week and 13-week EMAs, 12-26-9 MACD-lines and MACD-Histogram

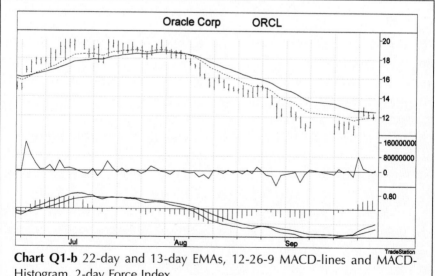

Chart Q1-b 22-day and 13-day EMAs, 12-26-9 MACD-lines and MACD-Histogram, 2-day Force Index

Mark at least two trading signals on the weekly as well as the daily charts, and make a trading decision at the right edge. Do not turn this page or look at the Answers pages until you have documented your decision.   Answer on pages 164–165.

Trade 1: Oracle Corp   ORCL—*Exit Question*

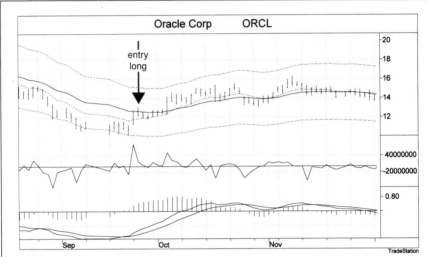

Chart Q1-c 22-day and 13-day EMAs, channel, 12-26-9 MACD-lines and MACD-Histogram, and 2-day Force Index

You do not get paid for entering trades, you get paid for exiting them. Beginners spend most of their time looking for trades, but give little thought to how they will exit. It is a fact that most trades are profitable at some point, yet despite that, most beginners lose money on most trades. They lose because they fail to exit at the right time.

This exercise is designed to help you learn to find exit and reentry points. Cover this chart with a sheet of paper so that you can see only from its left edge to the point where you entered the trade. Start moving the sheet of paper slowly to the right. Uncover one day at a time and stop to look and analyze what you see. If you think that you see a good exit point, mark it on the chart. Later, on the Answers pages, you will see several exit and reentry points. You will be able to compare notes and grade yourself.

Answer on pages 166–167.

Trade 2: Sun Microsystems   SUNW—*Entry Question*

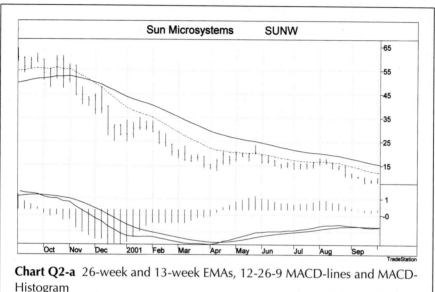

Chart Q2-a 26-week and 13-week EMAs, 12-26-9 MACD-lines and MACD-Histogram

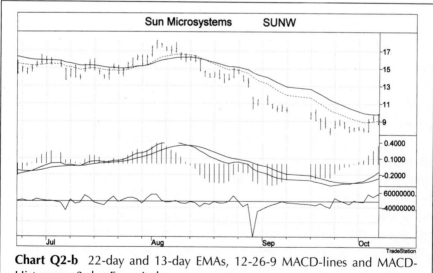

Chart Q2-b 22-day and 13-day EMAs, 12-26-9 MACD-lines and MACD-Histogram, 2-day Force Index

Mark at least two trading signals on the weekly as well as the daily charts and make a trading decision at the right edge. Do not turn this page or look at the Answers pages until you have documented your decision.   Answer on pages 168–169.

Trade 2: Sun Microsystems   SUNW—*Exit Question*

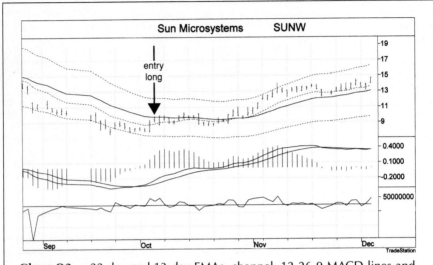

Chart Q2-c 22-day and 13-day EMAs, channel, 12-26-9 MACD-lines and MACD-Histogram, 2-day Force Index

Cover this chart with a sheet of paper and start moving it from left to right until you reach the vertical arrow, marking the day in October when we went long SUNW. Continue to uncover the chart, one day at a time. Analyze each day and mark exit and reentry points. Later, on the Answers pages, you will be able to compare notes and grade yourself.

Putting on a trade is like jumping into a fast-moving river. You have more control over an entry than over an exit. You can wait to jump in until you see a perfect or near-perfect point. Getting out is much harder because of the fast current and rocky shores. When you wait for an entry, your only risk is a missed opportunity, but there are many opportunities in the markets. Exits are much more demanding—you want to allow a stock to move in your favor to its full potential, but you do not want to risk losing your paper profits.

Answer on pages 170–171.

Trade 3: Kroll Inc   KROL—*Entry Question*

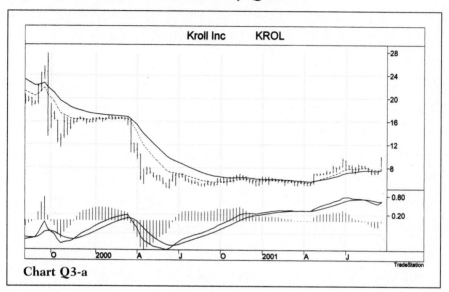

Chart Q3-a

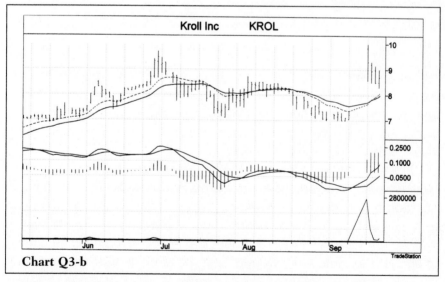

Chart Q3-b

This company provides corporate security, and it popped up on my "radar screen" shortly after the September 11 disaster.

Mark at least two trading signals on the weekly as well as the daily charts and make a trading decision at the right edge. Do not turn this page or look at the Answers pages until you have documented your decision.   Answer on pages 172–173.

Trade 3: Kroll Inc   KROL—*Exit Question*

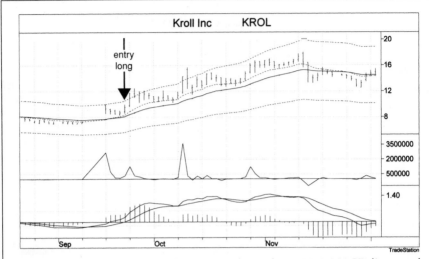

Chart Q3-c 22-day and 13-day EMAs, channel, 12-26-9 MACD-lines and MACD-Histogram, 2-day Force Index

As usual, cover this chart with a sheet of paper and move it slowly from left to right, one day at a time. Analyze each day and mark likely exit and reentry points—there are always several of those per trade. Later, on the Answers pages we will review them, and you will earn points for each correctly identified exit point.

We went long KROL in the area marked by an arrow in September. Now we have to decide where to get out of this trade. This is a difficult question in a trade that is based partly on fundamentals and partly on technical factors. The fundamental underpinnings mean that we have to give the bulls the benefit of the doubt and not be in too much of a hurry to exit. At the same time, we must put the ultimate trust in our technical indicators and use them to exit a trade.

Answer on pages 174–175.

Trade 4: Imclone Systems   IMCL—*Entry Question*

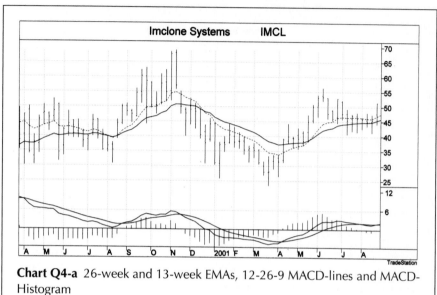

Chart Q4-a 26-week and 13-week EMAs, 12-26-9 MACD-lines and MACD-Histogram

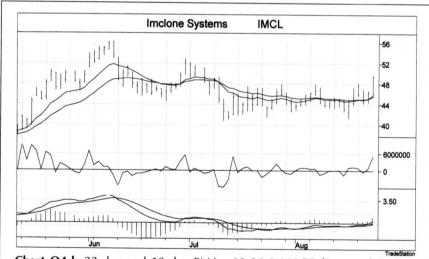

Chart Q4-b 22-day and 13-day EMAs, 12-26-9 MACD-lines and MACD-Histogram, 2-day Force Index

Imclone is a biopharmaceutical company, working on cancer treatments.

Answer on pages 176–177.

Trade 4: Imclone Systems   IMCL—*Exit Question*

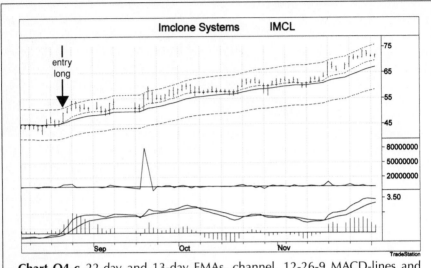

Chart Q4-c 22-day and 13-day EMAs, channel, 12-26-9 MACD-lines and MACD-Histogram, 2-day Force Index

Cover this chart with a sheet of paper and move it slowly from left to right, one day at a time. Mark entry and exit points and jot down a comment about each. Later, on the Answers pages, we will review them, and you'll earn points for each correctly identified exit or reentry point.

We went long IMCL in the area marked by an arrow in August. Chart patterns and indicator signals can help us decide where to take profits and where to reestablish longs. When you look at an old chart, the benefit of hindsight makes it seem very easy to hold for the long haul. If you cover up the chart and advance one day at a time, you will recreate some of the uncertainty and the psychological pressures of trading; taking short-term profits will suddenly look a lot more appealing.

Answer on pages 178–179.

Trade 5: Wheat—*Entry Question*

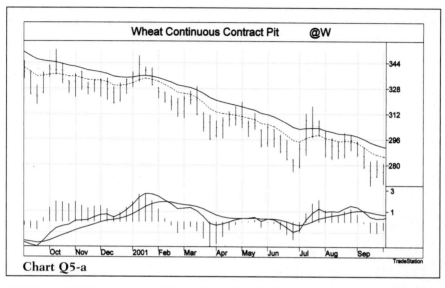

Chart Q5-a

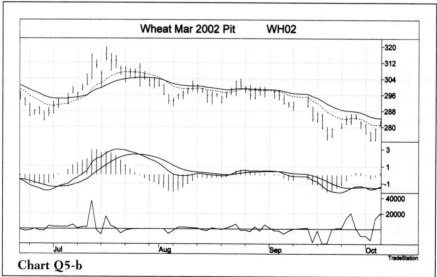

Chart Q5-b

The rules of technical analysis work in any freely traded market, including stocks, futures, and currencies—it can be applied to most trading vehicles. Many popular technical tools were originally developed for commodities and only later migrated to the stock market. Answer on pages 180–181.

Trade 5: Wheat—*Exit Question*

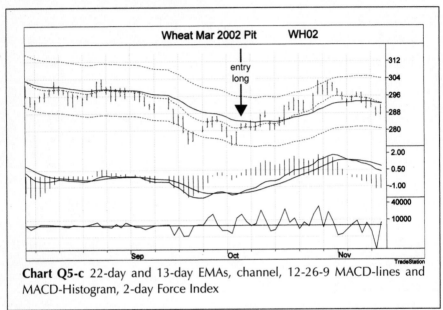

Chart Q5-c 22-day and 13-day EMAs, channel, 12-26-9 MACD-lines and MACD-Histogram, 2-day Force Index

The best way to test a trading system is by clicking through your data one day at a time. To learn from a chart, cover it with a sheet of paper, moving it from left to right, a day at a time. Mark all entry and exit points and jot down a comment about each. Later, on the Answers pages, you'll earn points for each correctly identified exit or reentry point.

We went long wheat in the area marked by an arrow in October. Use chart patterns and indicator signals to decide where to take profits and to reestablish longs. If you cover up the chart and advance one day at a time, you will recreate some of the uncertainties and pressures of trading.

Answer on pages 182–183.

Trade 6: Vimpel Communications   VIP—*Entry Question*

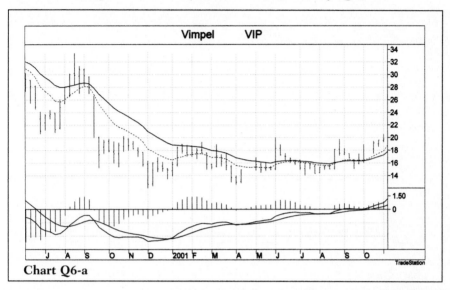

Chart Q6-a

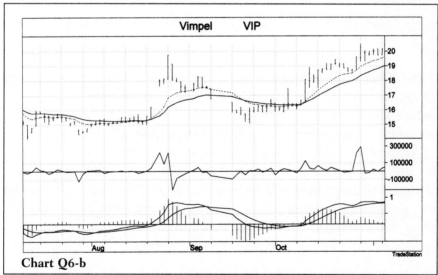

Chart Q6-b

Here's another set of charts that reflects the universality of technical analysis. The charts show a Russian stock listed on the NYSE—a cell phone company from Moscow. I sometimes think that when we trade VIP, comrades Lenin and Stalin take a few spins in their graves.

Mark at least two trading signals on the weekly and daily charts. Answer on pages 184–185.

Trade 6: Vimpel Communications   VIP—*Exit Question*

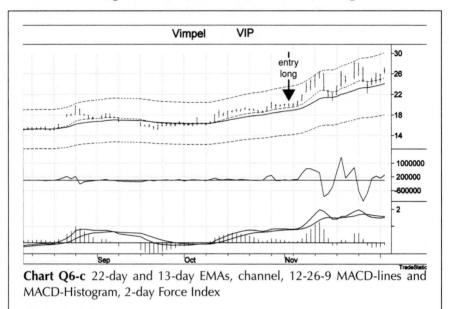

Chart Q6-c 22-day and 13-day EMAs, channel, 12-26-9 MACD-lines and MACD-Histogram, 2-day Force Index

Cover this chart with a sheet of paper and move it, one bar a time, from left to right. Mark all entry and exit points and jot down a comment about each. Once finished, review the Answers pages and award yourself points for each correctly identified exit or reentry point.

We went long VIP near the fast EMA, in the area marked by an arrow in October. Use chart patterns and indicator signals to decide where to take profits and where to reestablish longs. Covering up the chart and opening it up one day at a time allows you to recreate some of the pressure of trading this seemingly exotic stock.

Answer on pages 186–187.

Trade 7: International Business Machines   IBM—*Entry Question*

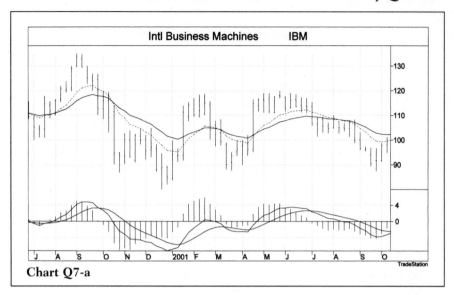

Chart Q7-a

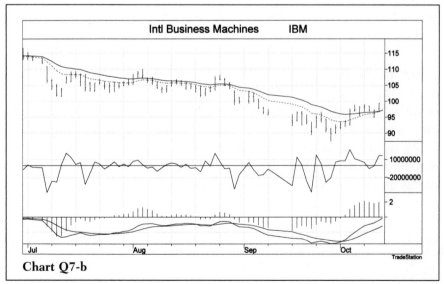

Chart Q7-b

IBM, "Big Blue", is widely held by institutions. It is a charter member of the blue chip club. It can swing, but it is unlikely to embark on a wild rally or suffer a bone-crashing decline like so many "cats and dogs."

Mark at least two trading signals on the weekly as well as the daily charts and make a trading decision at the right edge. Answer on pages 188–189.

Trade 7: International Business Machines IBM—*Exit Question*

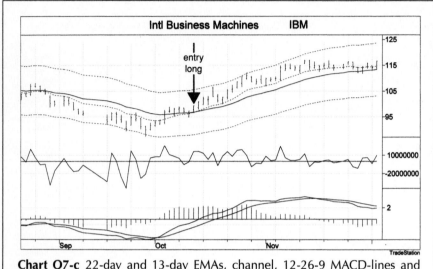

Chart Q7-c 22-day and 13-day EMAs, channel, 12-26-9 MACD-lines and MACD-Histogram, 2-day Force Index

Cover this chart with a sheet of paper and move it one bar at a time, from left to right. Identify entries, exits, and reentry points. Mark each of them and write a brief comment. Do not go to the Answers pages until you have finished this work.

We went long IBM near the fast EMA, in the area marked by an arrow in October. Keep tracking IBM one day at a time and find where to take profits and where to reestablish longs in this blue chip.

Answer on pages 190–191.

Trade 8: Biovail Corporation BVF—*Entry Question*

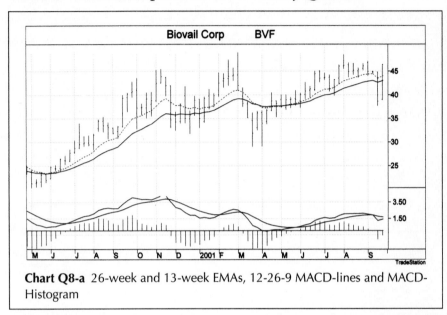

Chart Q8-a 26-week and 13-week EMAs, 12-26-9 MACD-lines and MACD-Histogram

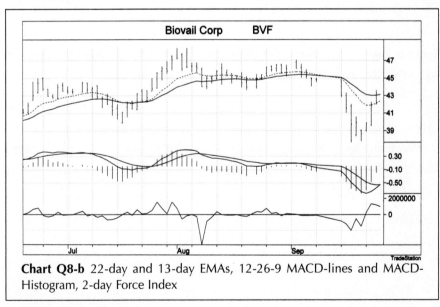

Chart Q8-b 22-day and 13-day EMAs, 12-26-9 MACD-lines and MACD-Histogram, 2-day Force Index

Mark at least two trading signals on the weekly as well as the daily charts and make a trading decision at the right edge. Do not turn this page or look at the Answers pages until you have documented your decision.   Answer on pages 192–193.

Trade 8: Biovail Corporation   BVF—*Exit Question*

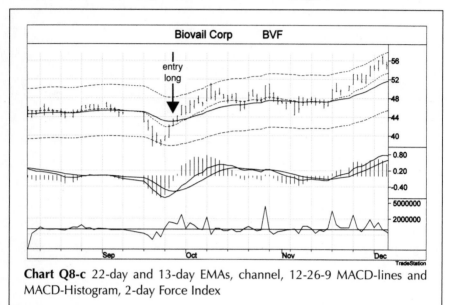

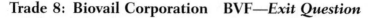

Chart Q8-c 22-day and 13-day EMAs, channel, 12-26-9 MACD-lines and MACD-Histogram, 2-day Force Index

Follow the usual pattern of covering this chart with a sheet of paper and moving it, one bar at a time, from left to right. After each new bar opens up, try to identify entries, exits, and reentry points. Mark each of them, write a brief comment, and when you finish working through the entire chart go to the Answers pages.

We went long BVF when it was straddling its EMAs, in the area marked by an arrow in September. Keep tracking BVF one day at a time and find where to take profits or reestablish longs.

Answer on pages 194–195.

LET'S TRADE: ANSWERS AND RATINGS

Trade 1: Oracle Corp   ORCL—*Entry Answer*
A Fallen Angel Ready to Fly

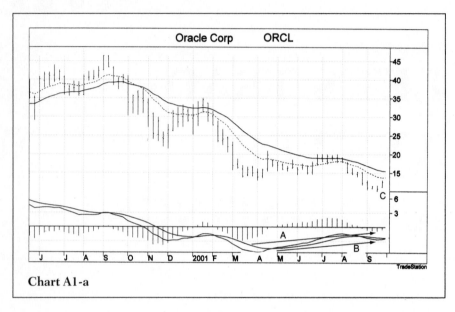

Chart A1-a

When the bull market in technology stocks ended in 2000, it gave way to a vicious bear market. Many weak companies were delisted and went bankrupt, but the decline also swept down shares of many well-run companies. Oracle is one of America's great technological corporations, not some silly dot-com. Still, its shares were taken down from a high of 46 in 2000 to a low of 10 in 2001, a nearly 80% decline.

In early October 2001, weekly MACD-Histogram ticked up from a higher bottom, completing a bullish divergence against a much lower bottom in May, while prices traced a lower bottom. The fast 13-week EMA turned flat. Even though the longer-term 26-week EMA continued to decline, a bullish divergence of MACD-Histogram allowed us to override the signal of the EMA.

The daily chart sports two bullish divergences. MACD-Histogram keeps tracing more and more shallow bottoms, which show that bears are becoming weaker even as prices grind lower. The more shallow bottoms of Force Index confirm that bears are running out of steam.

The blank area in September marks the week when the market was closed, following the September 11th disaster. After the market reopened,

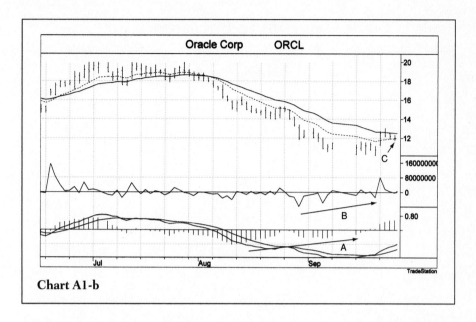

Chart A1-b

many stocks went into a tailspin, but ORCL just flirted with the new lows for a few days before rallying. During that rally, Force Index rose to its highest peak since June, confirming that this stock was completely sold out, bears had no more power, and the next move was likely to be up.

Entry Ratings

WEEKLY CHART
A—Bullish divergence of MACD-Histogram: 1 point
B—Bullish divergence of MACD-lines: 1 point
C—Price below the EMA, in the undervalued zone: 1 point

DAILY CHART
A—Bullish divergence of MACD-Histogram: 1 point
B—Bullish divergence of Force Index: 1 point
C—Rising 13-day EMA, price in the value zone between fast and slow EMAs: 1 point

DECISION
Go long ORCL, with a stop below the month's low, and observe money management rules: 3 points.

PASS POINT 6

Trade 1: Oracle Corp   ORCL—*Exit Answer*

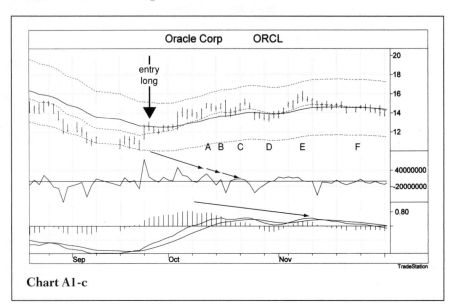

Chart A1-c

ORCL wasted little time before rallying above its moving averages. The failure of the rally to reach the upper channel line lets you know that the upmove is not likely to be very strong. The channel has been drawn to contain the data during the decline in September. Back then, declines used to punch the lower channel line. Now, the failure of prices to reach the upper channel line shows that the rally is weak and profits should be taken quickly instead of waiting for more, which you would do in a powerful rally.

At point A, Force Index has completed a triple bearish divergence— three lower tops during three uplegs of a rally. Prices still cannot reach the upper channel line, making this a good spot to take profits and employ your cash and attention elsewhere. The divergence deepens at point B and gives a final ring at point C, after Force Index rises above its centerline following the first nasty spill since the beginning of the rally.

Overstaying a long trade in area C would have meant sitting through an unpleasant decline below the EMA. That decline D actually creates another buying opportunity, followed by a bearish divergence of MACD-Histogram in area E—a lower indicator peak during a higher price peak.

A trader who oversleeps exit E gets one last chance in area F, where the EMAs scream to sell when they turn down. Holding longs beyond that point is strictly for losers.

Exit Ratings

DAILY CHART A-1C
Sell longs in area A: 3 points
Sell longs in area B: 2 points
Sell longs in area C: 2 points
Reposition long in area D: 2 points
Sell longs in area E: 3 points
Sell longs in area F: 1 point

PASS POINT 7

Why do some casinos give players bonuses for spending more time at the tables? They know that the longer you stay, the more likely you are to leave your money in the casino. The best trades are fairly short. You identify an island of order in the ocean of disorder, put on a trade to capitalize on it, quickly pocket your winnings, and go looking for another trade. There is no ideal exit, but generally, a fast exit is better than a slow one.

Trade 2: Sun Microsystems   SUNW—*Entry Answer*
Sold Down to Rock Bottom

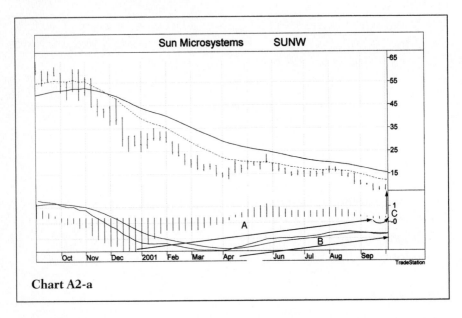

Chart A2-a

This is another "fallen angel"—a high flier blown out of the sky by the bear market in high-tech stocks. Many poor souls were desperate enough to buy SUNW at 65, but few buyers came when SUNW hit its 7.50 low. The average height of a bar reflects the level of trading activity. The bars were much taller above 60 than below 10, reflecting greater public interest in this stock near the top than near the bottom.

At the right edge of the weekly chart, MACD-Histogram has completed a bullish divergence A by ticking up from a much more shallow bottom in 2001 than it reached in 2000, even though prices are much lower. Moreover, there is a rarely seen bullish divergence B of MACD-lines between the April and September bottoms. In area C, prices are undervalued, below the EMA, and the latest bar of MACD-Histogram, while pointing down, is shorter than the previous bar. This uptick completes a bullish divergence, telling us to look for an entry into a long trade on the daily charts.

The daily chart shows a bullish divergence A between Force Index and price, reflecting the weakness of bears during the late September

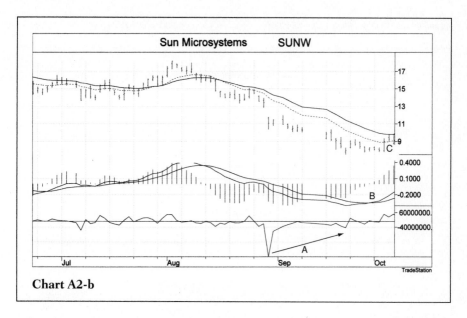

Chart A2-b

low. In area B, both MACD-Histogram and MACD-lines are rising, confirming the strength of the bulls. At the right edge of the chart, in area C, the fast EMA is already rising, a bullish sign. The slow EMA is still flat, with prices in the value area between the two EMAs.

Entry Ratings

WEEKLY CHART

A—Bullish divergence of MACD-Histogram: 1 point
B—Bullish divergence of MACD-lines: 1 point
C—Price below the EMA, in the undervalued zone: 1 point

DAILY CHART

A—Bullish divergence of Force Index: 1 point
B—Rising MACD-Histogram and MACD-lines: 1 point
C—Rising 13-day EMA, price in the value zone between fast and
   slow EMAs: 1 point

DECISION

Go long SUNW, with a stop below the month's low, and observe
   money management rules: 3 points.

PASS POINT 6

Trade 2: Sun Microsystems   SUNW—*Exit Answer*

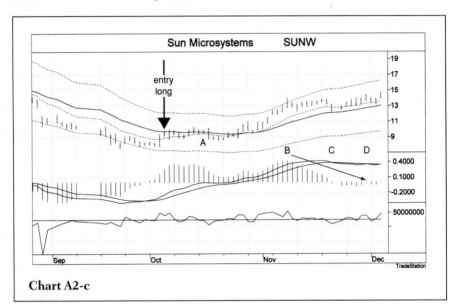

Chart A2-c

As a rule, it pays to bracket the long moving average with an envelope or a channel and use its walls as guidelines for taking profits. One of the few proven behaviors of the market is its tendency to oscillate above and below value. If we buy near the moving average, near value, then our goal is to sell when the stock or commodity becomes overvalued, near the upper channel line.

The first selling opportunity in SUNW comes in area A, after the stock spends more than a week going nowhere, straddling its moving average. Do we want to give the trade more time to work out, or close it and look for another? If you trade a small account, it is important to free up your capital. Even in a larger account, a stock that is going nowhere ties up more than capital. It competes for the trader's attention, taking his mind off other, more promising, trades, almost like a sick child tends to get the lion's share of attention in the family.

If we continue to hold, SUNW presents a fantastic selling opportunity in area B. Prices speed up to the upside, puncture the upper channel line with an unusually tall bar, only to weaken near the close and end the day within the channel. Our goal is to sell above value, and this stab above the upper channel line shows that the market is overvalued but cannot hold that level. MACD-Histogram ticks down the next day, confirming that bulls are running out of breath.

A quick stab into the area between the two EMAs around Thanksgiving, in area C, creates a buying opportunity since the weekly chart still is in an uptrend. In area D, SUNW rises to a double top, while MACD-Histogram traces a bearish divergence and gives a strong sell signal. Prices fail to reach their upper channel line, while MACD-Histogram diverges and even MACD-lines start to diverge. There is no point in sticking around any longer; it is high time to take your winnings off the table and switch your attention to another stock.

Exit Ratings

DAILY CHART A-2c

Sell longs in area A: 3 points
Sell longs in area B: 5 points
Reposition long in area C: 3 points
Sell longs in area D: 3 points

PASS POINT 8

Trade 3: Kroll Inc   KROL—*Entry Answer*
KROL—On the Front Burner

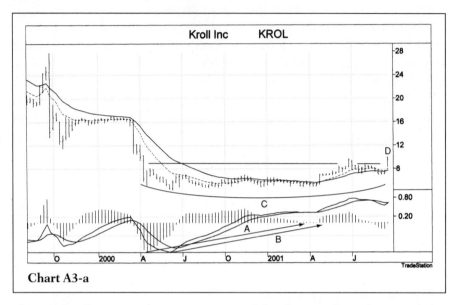

Chart A3-a

This trade illustrates the importance of fundamental analysis and the value of personal networking. Shortly after the September 11 disaster, a group of campers gathered for our regular monthly meeting in my Manhattan apartment. We agreed that the investment/trading theme for the next several months was likely to be security and I asked one of our campers to come up with a complete list of all security-related firms. I reviewed each of them, using the Triple Screen system. KROL appeared to be the most attractive stock on the list, and I e-mailed my analysis to everyone who was at our meeting.

Kroll, Inc. is an international corporate security firm. Its stock traded above 41 in 1999 before sliding below 5 in 2000 when it made a few unwise acquisitions. In 2001 it appeared completely sold out and listless, with narrow weekly ranges. MACD-Histogram and MACD-lines have traced bullish divergences A and B, while prices have traced a rounded bottom, known as a "saucer bottom" C, with a breakout at D.

The daily chart shows an upside gap immediately after the resumption of trading in September, followed by a brief pullback. The huge peak of Force Index, which makes its entire previous history appear as a flat line, shows a tremendous bullish force and calls for higher prices ahead. Both

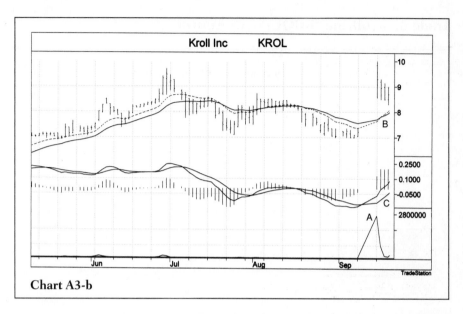

Chart A3-b

moving averages are rising at the right edge—bullish. MACD-Histogram and MACD-lines are also rising, confirming the bullish power.

Entry Ratings

WEEKLY CHART

A—Bullish divergence of MACD-Histogram: 1 point
B—Bullish divergence of MACD-lines: 1 point
C—Price below the EMA, in the undervalued zone: 1 point
D—Breakout: 1 point

DAILY CHART

A—Bullish upswing of Force Index: 1 point
B—Rising MACD-Histogram and MACD-lines: 1 point
C—Rising 13-day and 22-day EMAs: 1 point

DECISION

Go long KROL, with a stop at the upper edge of the gap and observe money management rules: 3 points.

Alternatively, wait to buy when a daily low touches the fast EMA, and adjust buy orders daily: 3 points.

The reason we may consider buying KROL this high is that the market underwent a sudden and massive fundamental change.

PASS POINT 7

Trade 3: Kroll Inc KROL—*Exit Answer*

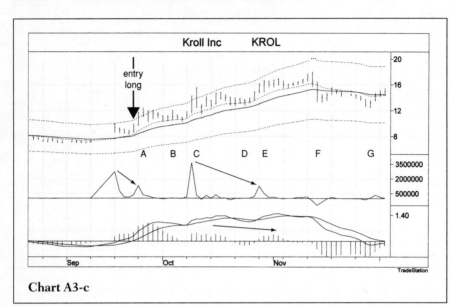

Chart A3-c

The first selling opportunity in KROL comes in the area A, where the stock penetrates its channel, while Force Index traces a bearish divergence. There is a great reentry opportunity in area B, when KROL returns to its fast EMA. We need to calculate this EMA daily, estimate its value for tomorrow, and put our buy order in that area.

The rally in area C offers us a choice—take profits above the envelope or continue to hold because peak C of Force Index is even higher than peak A. When bulls grow stronger as prices rise, they tell us that higher prices are likely ahead.

The pullback to the EMA in area D presents another good opportunity to reestablish long positions or to add to existing ones. The rally in area E creates the best exit opportunity for longs—bearish divergence C-E of Force Index shows that bulls are running out of steam, while the failure of prices to reach their upper channel line confirms this message. MACD-Histogram also traces a bearish divergence, in tandem with Force Index. It is the end of the game for the bulls, the bells are ringing, warning you that the uptrend is ready to reverse.

The sharp drop in area F must hit any sensible stop-loss or protect-profit order. Both EMAs turn down in area G, screaming to sell. But this exit is strictly for the beginners who goofed and missed much more profitable earlier exits.

Exit Ratings

DAILY CHART A-3c

Sell longs in area A: 3 points
Hold longs in area A: 3 points
Add to longs in area B: 3 points
Sell longs in area C: 3 points
Hold longs in area C: 3 points
Add to longs in area D: 3 points
Sell longs in area E: 5 points
Sell longs in area F: 1 point
Sell longs in area G: 1 point

PASS POINT 13

Trade 4: Imclone Systems IMCL—*Entry Answer*
IMCL: A Steady Trend Against a Pervasive Enemy

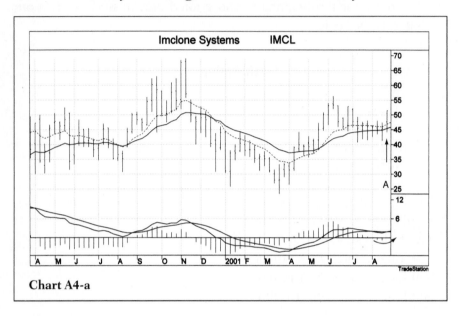

Chart A4-a

A key principle of the Triple Screen trading system is to make strategic decisions on long-term charts, and then turn to short-term charts for tactical decisions about entries and exits. The weekly chart of IMCL shows a series of slow and steady swings, each lasting several months. If we can get in gear with an upswing, we should trade from the long side as long as it continues. If we get in gear with a downswing, we can continue shorting for as long as that downmove stays in force.

At the right edge of the weekly chart, in area A, both weekly EMAs have turned up, giving buy signals. At the same time, MACD-Histogram has ticked up, reinforcing the bullish message (this is an Impulse System buy—both the EMA and MACD-Histogram point higher).

IMCL has been stuck in a flat trading range for the past two months. The bottoms of MACD-Histogram have become shallow, showing that bears are becoming weaker. Bulls, at the same time, have maintained their strength—the rallies of MACD-Histogram above its centerline have been rising to the same level during those two months. As prices push higher, toward overhead resistance near the right edge, Force Index

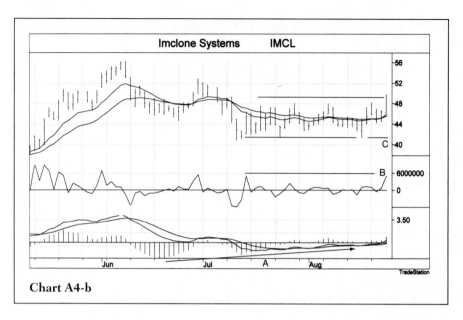

Chart A4-b

rises to a new multimonth high, confirming bullish strength. At the same time, prices punch up through the resistance, closing above that level. This breakout turns resistance into support, which is likely to create a bottom under any decline.

Entry Ratings

WEEKLY CHART
A—An uptick of MACD-Histogram: 1 point
A—An uptick of both moving averages: 1 point

DAILY CHART
A—Bullish upswing of MACD-Histogram: 1 point
B—New high of Force Index: 1 point
C—Upside breakout through overhead resistance: 1 point

DECISION
Go long IMCL, with a stop below the previous day's low, and observe money management rules: 3 points.
Alternatively, wait to buy when the low of a daily bar touches the fast EMA; keep adjusting buy orders daily: 3 points.

PASS POINT 6

Trade 4: Imclone Systems   IMCL—*Exit Answer*

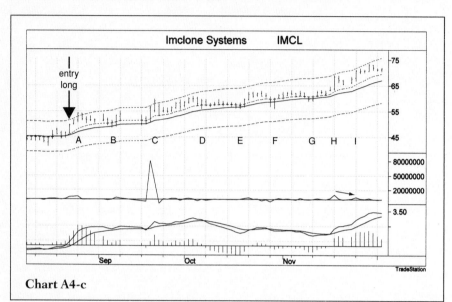

Chart A4-c

IMCL offers a profit-taking opportunity at point A, just two days after the entry. Prices blow outside of their channel, marking an overbought condition, a selling opportunity. A decline that follows takes IMCL down into the "sweet zone"—the value area between the fast and the slow EMAs.

There is a window in September—a blank spot following the suspension of trading after the terrorist acts of September 11. Most stocks sank after the markets reopened, but not IMCL. Two days later Force Index rallies to a fantastic peak, indicating a great buildup of buying pressure. When a stock bucks the trend of the market, it sends a strong message that it really wants to go its way, no matter what.

There is a decision to be made in area C—to take profits above the envelope or to continue to hold. The great height of peak C of Force Index indicates that higher prices are likely ahead because bulls grow stronger as prices rise.

If you sell, IMCL provides a new buying opportunity in area D, where it declines below its fast EMA, and an even better opportunity in area E. The volatility decreases, and prices stay for a few days in that value zone between the two EMAs, before embarking on a new rally.

That rally, and the following one, starting from the bottom F, are decidedly anemic affairs. IMCL is still trending higher, but losing its old vigor. When the rally H approaches the upper channel line, it offers a chance to take profits. There is one final good exit, in area I, where a bearish divergence of Force Index is shouting to sell.

Exit Ratings

DAILY CHART A-4c

Sell longs in area A: 3 points
Hold longs in area A: 3 points
Add to longs in area B: 3 points
Sell longs in area C: 3 points
Add to longs in area D: 3 points
Add to longs in area E: 3 points
Add to longs in area F: 1 point
Add to longs in area G: 1 point
Sell longs in area H: 3 points
Sell longs in area I: 3 points

PASS POINT 14

Trade 5: Wheat—*Entry Answer*
Wheat—Everybody Eats It

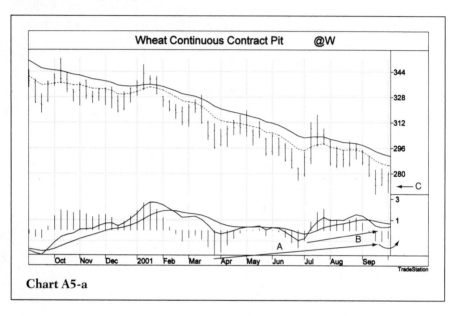

Chart A5-a

Commodities are the essential building blocks of the economy. Nobody really needs a share of amazon.com—it may be a nice speculation, but if AMZN disappears, somebody else will sell books and we'll find something else to trade. On the other hand, we could not live our normal lives without wheat, cotton, sugar, or other commodities.

Since commodity contracts expire every few months, we need to use perpetual or continuous contracts to analyze long-term weekly charts. Those are mathematical constructs that combine the nearby actual contracts in a seamless transition. We use real contracts to study the daily charts.

At the right edge of the weekly chart, wheat appears to be at the tail end of a multiyear bear market—it is the cheapest it has been in more than a decade. Both EMAs are declining, but MACD-Histogram is flashing the only signal that can override the message of the EMAs—a bullish divergence between the indicator and price. There is also a bullish divergence by MACD-lines, rarely seen on the weekly charts.

At the right edge of the daily chart, wheat has just penetrated a historic low, set a week ago, earlier in September. Wheat failed to follow

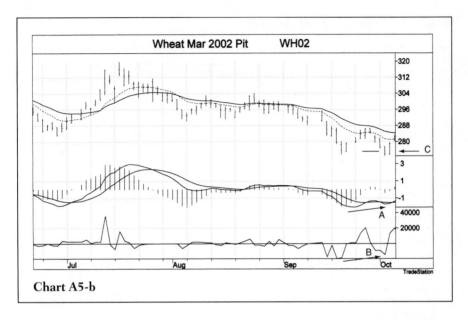

Chart A5-b

through on that downside breakout and ticked up instead. Both MACD-Histogram and MACD-lines, as well as Force Index, have traced bullish divergences—higher indicator bottoms at a time when prices traced a deeper bottom. This is an excellent buying opportunity, with a tight stop immediately below the latest lows.

Entry Ratings

WEEKLY CHART

A—Bullish divergence of MACD-Histogram: 1 point

B—Bullish divergence of MACD-lines: 1 point

C—Price below value, below both moving averages: 1 point

DAILY CHART

A—Bullish divergence of MACD-Histogram: 1 point

A—Bullish divergence of MACD-lines: 1 point

B—Bullish divergence of Force Index: 1 point

C—False downside breakout: 1 point

DECISION

Go long wheat, with a stop below the current week's low, and observe money management rules: 3 points.

PASS POINT 7

Trade 5: Wheat—*Exit Answer*

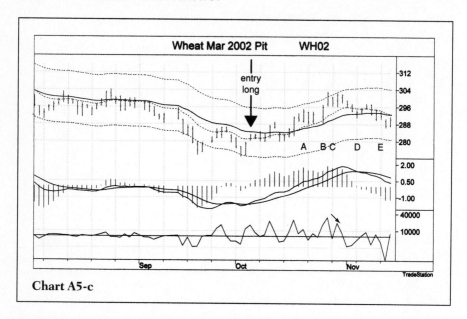

Chart A5-c

Wheat slowly gathers steam, as it starts rallying from its multiyear low. Its daily ranges are narrow and prices do not outrun the EMAs very far. Slow rallies tend to persist longer than wild affairs. Still, it would be tempting to take profits in area A, after wheat manages to put some air between itself and its moving averages.

Area B offers a good opportunity to reestablish longs or to add to the existing ones when wheat pokes into the value zone between the two EMAs. A conscientious trader calculates his EMAs daily, projects them one day ahead, and places his entry orders accordingly.

After touching its EMAs in area B, wheat explodes into area C, where it offers a perfect profit-taking opportunity. Prices blow out of their channel into overvalued territory, accompanied by a bearish divergence of Force Index, which shows that prices are rising only out of inertia, as bulls have less force.

Prices sink back to their EMAs in area D, tempting traders to reposition long; only instead of rallying they continue to sink, hitting stops. In area E both EMAs turn down, canceling the buy signal altogether. This is the end of the bullish campaign in wheat for the time being.

Nobody can know the future with certainty. All we can do is play the probabilities, buy at the rising EMA, and take profits in the vicinity of the upper channel line, all the while protecting our positions with stops. We may move stops only in the direction of the trade, never against it.

Exit Ratings

DAILY CHART A-5C

Sell longs in area A: 3 points
Add to longs in area B: 3 points
Sell longs in area C: 5 points
Add to longs in area D: 3 points
Cancel buy orders and liquidate any remaining longs in area E: 3 points

PASS POINT 9

Trade 6: Vimpel Communications VIP—*Entry Answer*
VIP—Rubles to Dollars

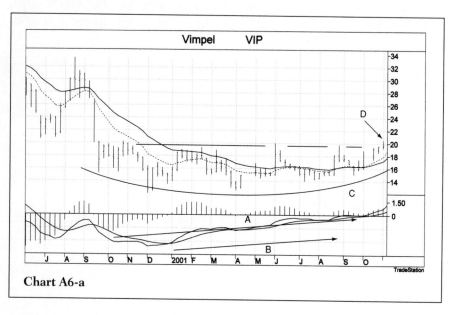

Chart A6-a

We can apply technical analysis to markets in all countries because of the essential similarity of human beings. The veneer of civilization gives us different appearances, but underneath we are all wired the same way. When people feel stressed, their behavior patterns are remarkably similar across cultural divides. Technical analysis picks up the behavior of people under stress. If you had not known that VIP was a Russian stock, you would have analyzed it in the same way as any other stock on your list.

VIP had its IPO in the high 20's and then twice stabbed at the 60 level before sinking in the 2000–2001 bear market. Once it slid below 20, several technical patterns began to emerge, which eventually coalesced into a trading signal at the right edge of the chart.

MACD-Histogram has traced a long-term bullish divergence A, followed by a bullish divergence B of MACD-lines. Prices have traced a "saucer bottom" that held all the declines, and a flat top that knocked back rallies. Finally, at point D, prices broke through that resistance. EMAs, MACD-Histogram, and MACD-lines turned higher at that point.

At the right edge of the daily chart, VIP has broken above its August peak and is holding that level, refusing to decline. The breakout was

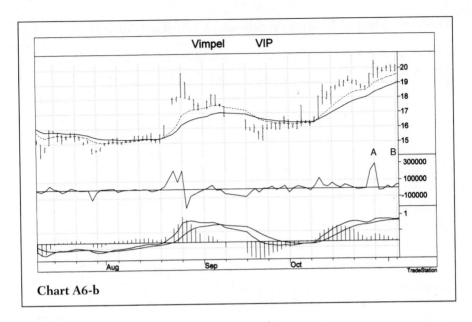

Chart A6-b

confirmed by peak A in Force Index whose highest reading in several months called for higher prices ahead. Can we call the pattern of MACD-Histogram a bearish divergence? No, because it never declined below the centerline between the two peaks—it is merely a broad, powerful top. At point B both EMAs are rising, confirming the power of bulls.

Entry Ratings

WEEKLY CHART

A—Bullish divergence of MACD-Histogram: 1 point
B—Bullish divergence of MACD-lines: 1 point
C—Saucer bottom: 1 point
D—Upside breakout, confirmed by uptrending EMAs, MACD-Histogram, and MACD-lines: 1 point

DAILY CHART

A—Record peak of Force Index: 1 point
B—Rising EMAs: 1 point

DECISION

Go long VIP at the fast EMA, with a stop below the week's low, and observe money management rules: 3 points.

PASS POINT 6

Trade 6: Vimpel Communications VIP—*Exit Answer*

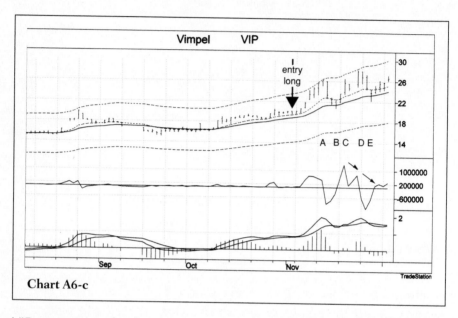

Chart A6-c

VIP starts rising slowly, retreating to its EMA and giving traders a chance to get long near value. It gathers steam and hits its upper channel line in area A, where Force Index rises to a new multimonth high. That is a sign of the great force of bulls, pointing to the likelihood of higher prices ahead. That peak makes it very tempting to hold through whatever decline may lay ahead. Still, there is no harm in selling and looking to reposition long when the stock sinks back near value in the area of its fast EMA.

In area B, VIP declines into "the sweet zone" between the two EMAs; its daily ranges shrink, as lower prices do not attract traders' attention. Prices pop up in area C, then retreat without reaching the upper channel line. The next rally, in area D, provides a superb selling opportunity. Prices reach the upper channel line, an overvalued area. At the same time, Force Index, which had been calling for higher and higher prices, traces a bearish divergence C-D. It shows that bulls are running out of steam, and the rally is close to its top.

Prices stab below the slow EMA and offer another buying opportunity in area E before embarking on a new upleg of rally. One of the key differences between professionals and amateurs is that the pros recognize signals early, while they are still a bit fuzzy and indistinct. An amateur keeps waiting for clear and certain signals. By the time those emerge, a trade is ripe for a reversal.

There are two main types of risk—money risk and information risk. An amateur is quick to accept money risks as he enters well-established trends where stops are far away, but the trend is pretty clear and the information risk is low. Professionals, on the other hand, are much more at ease with the information risk, acting in the atmosphere of uncertainty, as long as their money risks are low.

Exit Ratings

DAILY CHART A-6C

Sell longs in area A: 3 points
Add to longs in area B: 3 points
Sell longs in area C: 3 points
Sell longs in area D: 5 points
Buy longs in area E: 3 points

PASS POINT 9

Trade 7: International Business Machines IBM—*Entry Answer*
IBM—Steady Green from Big Blue

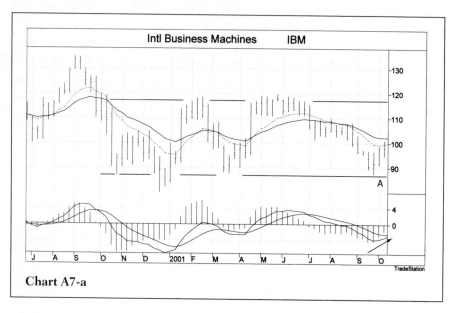

Intl Business Machines   IBM

Chart A7-a

Even a quick glance at this chart reveals that IBM has spent the past several years in a broad trading range. Whenever it declines below 90, it is time to look for a bottom, and whenever it rallies towards 120, it is time to look for a top.

At the right edge of the chart, in area A, IBM has recoiled from support and is headed higher. This rally is confirmed by the uptick of weekly MACD-Histogram. Note that there is no bullish divergence, simply an upside reversal of prices and the indicator. The fast EMA has already turned up, confirming the rally and giving an Impulse buy signal, while the slower EMA has gone flat, a normal behavior at an early stage of a rally.

The daily chart of IBM shows increased volatility following the September interruption of trading on the NYSE. By the end of that month, Force Index traces a bullish divergence A—a more shallow bottom of the indicator during a deeper price bottom. The new high of Force Index in area B calls for higher prices ahead; this message is confirmed by the uptrend of MACD in area C. The uptrend is further

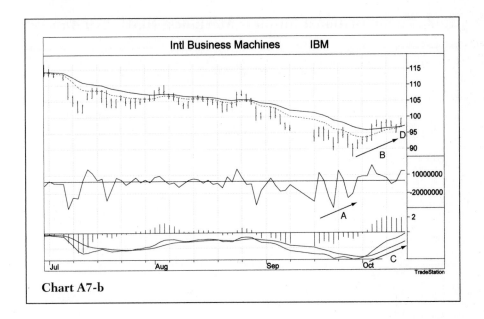

Chart A7-b

confirmed when both EMAs turn up at the right edge of the chart in area
D. The low of the last daily bar still touches both EMAs, a value area.

Entry Ratings

WEEKLY CHART
A—Bullish uptrend of MACD-Histogram: 1 point
A—Uptrend confirmed by the rising fast EMA: 1 point

DAILY CHART
A—Bullish divergence of Force Index: 1 point
B—Record peak of Force Index: 1 point
C—Uptrend of MACD: 1 point
D—Rising EMAs: 1 point

DECISION
Go long IBM near the fast EMA, with a stop below the week's low,
and observe money management rules: 3 points.

PASS POINT 6

Trade 7: International Business Machines IBM—*Exit Answer*

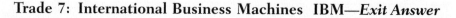

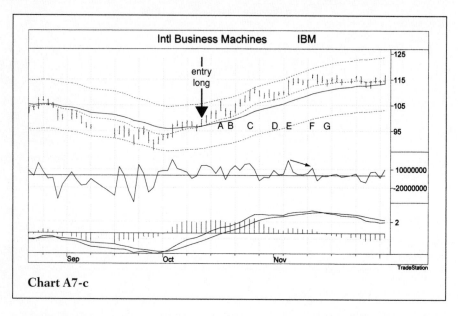

Chart A7-c

IBM is a typical blue chip, moving slowly and steadily, with none of the wild gyrations seen in so many "cats and dogs." The slope of the slow 22-day EMA tracks the trend, while the faster 13-day EMA identifies value levels for entries.

At point A, IBM rises near its upper channel line, offering the first of many selling opportunities. Two days later it backs down, touching the fast EMA. This pullback to value provides an excellent opportunity to hop aboard if you missed the first buy signal. Professional traders who have plenty of experience carrying large positions often use such pullbacks for pyramiding. They keep adding to their original positions, building them to a larger size, until they get an extra-strong exit signal, at which point they sell the whole lot.

The rally in area C provides another opportunity to take profits, as prices touch their upper channel line, an overvalued area. That rally is followed by a decline back to the EMA in area D, offering yet another opportunity to go long. This is the beauty of trading swings in blue chips. All you need to do is find a few stocks that exhibit regular swings, fine-tune your EMAs and channels, and start buying value and selling overvalued levels or shorting value and covering undervalued levels.

IBM rises into area E but fails to reach its upper channel line, a sign of lessening bullish power. If you miss this signal to sell, IBM rings a loud bell a few days later in area F. Another rally fails to reach the upper channel line, signifying weakness. At the same time, Force Index traces a bearish divergence E-F, calling for more weakness ahead. This is the type of strong sell signal that professionals await before banging out of their entire positions.

IBM offers yet another opportunity to get long, in area G, near the EMA, but it is very questionable whether we should take that signal. The trend is still rising, but going long so soon after a bearish divergence is seldom a good idea because more weakness can be expected. From that point onward, IBM goes flat, tying up a trader's capital and, more perniciously, his attention, which could be more profitably invested in other stocks.

Exit Ratings

DAILY CHART A-7C

Sell longs in area A: 3 points
Add to longs in area B: 3 points
Sell longs in area C: 3 points
Add to longs in area D: 3 points
Sell longs in area E: 3 points
Sell longs in area F: 5 points
Add to longs in area G: 1 point

PASS POINT 11

Trade 8: Biovail Corporation BVF—*Entry Answer*
BVF—Bull Market Punctuated by Sharp Breaks

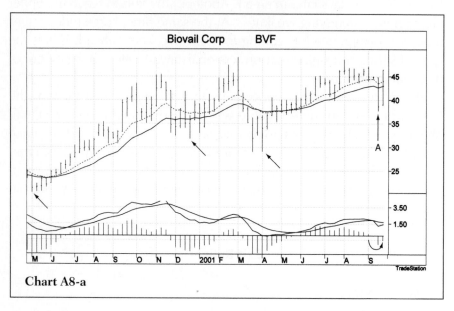

Chart A8-a

This chart shows a private bull market in BVF. The stock is moving from the lower left to the upper right corner of the chart while most other stocks are in the midst of a broad bear market. This uptrend is occasionally penetrated by sharp downdrafts, which do enough damage in a few weeks to wipe out the gains of several months.

To a beginner who comes late to the bullish party, each of those downdrafts can spell disaster. A pro, familiar with the past, is more likely to view those declines as buying opportunities. He is also likely to be extra careful with stops, protecting himself from sudden downmoves.

At the right edge of the chart, in area A, BVF has recovered from its post-September 11 dip. It has cleaned out weak bulls and is ready to resume its uptrend. The upmove is confirmed by an uptick of weekly MACD-Histogram, and an upturn of both weekly EMAs.

The daily chart of BVF shows increased downward volatility after the September 11 trading halt. The stock takes out its July low, but there is no follow-through to that breakout, which is a bullish sign. Within a

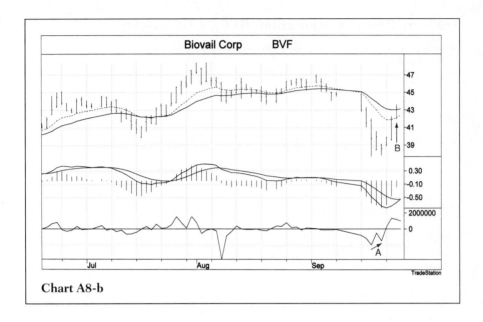

Chart A8-b

week, an even stronger bullish sign appears—a positive divergence of Force Index. It makes a more shallow second low, even as prices continue to pound their lows, below 39. The rally following the decline is very sharp, turning up both EMAs at the right edge of the chart—another bullish sign.

Entry Ratings

WEEKLY CHART
A—Uptick of MACD-Histogram: 1 point
A—Uptrend confirmed by the rising EMAs: 1 point

DAILY CHART
A—Bullish divergence of Force Index: 1 point
B—Rising EMAs: 1 point

DECISION
Go long BVF near the fast EMA, with a stop below the week's low, and observe money management rules: 3 points.

PASS POINT 5

Trade 8: Biovail Corporation BVF—*Exit Answer*

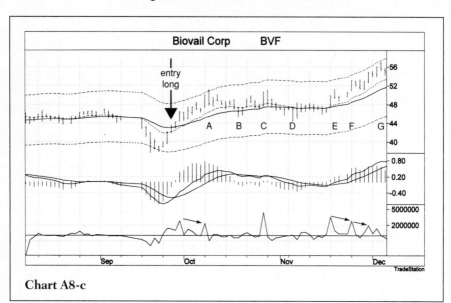

Chart A8-c

BVF shoots out of the gate in September and runs until it reaches the upper channel line, the profit-taking area, while Force Index traces a bearish divergence in area A. Notice a less distinct divergence a few days earlier. When a beginning trader faces such a pattern, he is better off taking profits early, while a more experienced trader may elect to hold. An important early step in a trader's development is learning to take profits without kicking himself for having left some money on the table. Learning to hold for a maximum gain is a skill that is best learned later.

Biovail sinks below its slow EMA in area B, offering an opportunity to get long below value. The stock rallies again in area C, and even though that rally never reaches the upper channel line, an extremely high peak of Force Index reveals the power of bulls and calls for higher prices ahead. If you took profits in area C, fine; if you decided to hold, even better, because such extreme peaks of Force Index show that bulls are very strong and higher prices are likely ahead.

BVF sinks below its EMAs in area D—notice its repetitive behavior in penetrating the EMA. Once you recognize such a pattern, put your buy order as many points below the EMA as the average depth of past penetrations.

Biovail rallies again in areas E, F, and G. None of those rallies reach the upper channel line, reflecting the weakness of bulls. At the same time, Force Index starts tracing lower and lower peaks. Those bearish divergences indicate that the top is near. Look back at the record peak of Force Index in area C—it reflected great power of the bulls and called for higher rallies ahead. That forecast has now been fulfilled, and in areas F and G Force Index is giving an opposite message—that the top is at hand. Good technical indicators work like headlights on a car. They do not show you the entire way home, but light up enough of the distance ahead so that if you travel at a reasonable speed, you can anticipate the next turn in the road.

Exit Ratings

DAILY CHART A-8c

Sell longs in area A: 5 points
Add to longs in area B: 3 points
Sell longs in area C: 3 points
Add to longs in area D: 3 points
Sell longs in area E: 3 points
Sell longs in area F: 5 points
Add to longs in area G: 3 points

PASS POINT 13

THE ROAD AHEAD

You can learn to trade. To begin, you need some basic skills—discipline, risk tolerance, and facility with numbers. You need knowledge, which can be acquired through dedicated study. By working through the *Study Guide* you have proven that you have what it takes to grow into a successful trader.

Now is the time to put your time and energy into setting up your trading operation. Design a record-keeping system, establish money management rules, and write your trading plan. This calls for a lot of work, but many of us find trading a fantastically interesting challenge. The rewards, if you do it right, are nothing to sneeze at either.

I enjoyed creating these exercises. People who came to my Traders' Camps were the first to learn my methods, take the tests, and comment on them. I also want to thank two people who put their own projects aside to help me prepare this book. Fred Schutzman, a technical analyst and money manager in New York, is an old and loyal friend who took every test in this book, graded his performance, and then pointed out several questions and answers that had to be rephrased, rearranged, or clarified. When it comes to analysis and trading, no imperfection can slip by Fred! My oldest daughter Miriam, a journalist and a graduate student in Paris, went through my English with a red pen. English is my third language, and the little girl, who is actually no longer so little, is now fixing the English for the guy who used to read *The Little Engine That Could* to her at bedtime.

You have worked through this book, but closing it does not mean having to say good-bye. If I continue to run my Traders' Camps, you may come to spend a week during which we'll study and work on trading together. I look forward to hearing about your findings and concepts as much as sharing mine with you. I now return to my trading room and wish you success in yours.

Dr. Alexander Elder
New York
February 2002

SOURCES

Appel, Gerald. *Day-Trading with Gerald Appel* (video) (New York: Financial Trading, 1989).

Douglas, Mark. *The Disciplined Trader* (New York: New York Institute of Finance, 1990).

Edwards, Robert D., and John Magee. *Technical Analysis of Stock Trends* (1948) (New York: New York Institute of Finance, 1992).

Elder, Alexander. *Come Into My Trading Room: A Complete Guide to Trading* (New York: John Wiley & Sons, 2002).

Elder, Alexander. *Study Guide for Trading for a Living* (New York: John Wiley & Sons, 1993).

Elder, Alexander. *Trading for a Living* (New York: John Wiley & Sons, 1993).

Kaufman, Perry J. *Smarter Trading* (New York: McGraw-Hill, 1995).

LeBeau, Charles, and David W. Lucas. *Technical Traders Guide to Computer Analysis of the Futures Market* (New York: McGraw-Hill, 1991).

LeFevre, Edwin. *Reminiscences of a Stock Operator* (New York: George H. Doran Company, 1923).

McMillan, Lawrence G. *Options as a Strategic Investment,* 3rd ed. (New York: New York Institute of Finance, 1999).

Murphy, John J. *Technical Analysis of the Financial Markets* (Englewood Cliffs, NJ: Prentice-Hall, 1999).

Schabacker, Richard W. *Technical Analysis and Stock Market Profits* (1932) (London: Pearson Professional Limited, 1997).

Schwager, Jack D. *Technical Analysis of the Futures Markets* (New York: John Wiley & Sons, 1995).

Teweles, Richard J., and Frank J. Jones. *The Futures Game,* 3rd ed. (New York: McGraw-Hill, 1998).

Vince, Ralph. *Portfolio Management Formulas* (New York: John Wiley & Sons, 1990).

ABOUT THE AUTHOR

Alexander Elder, M.D., is a professional trader, living in New York. He is the author of *Trading for a Living* and the *Study Guide for Trading for a Living*, considered modern classics among traders. First published in 1993, these international best-sellers have been translated into Chinese, Dutch, French, German, Greek, Japanese, Korean, Polish, and Russian. He also wrote *Rubles to Dollars*, a book about the transformation of Russia.

Dr. Elder was born in Leningrad and grew up in Estonia, where he entered medical school at the age of 16. At 23, while working as a ship's doctor, he jumped a Soviet ship in Africa and received political asylum in the United States. He worked as a psychiatrist in New York City and taught at Columbia University. His experience as a psychiatrist provided him with a unique insight into the psychology of trading. Dr. Elder's books, articles, and software reviews have established him as one of today's leading experts on trading.

Dr. Elder is a sought-after speaker at conferences and the originator of Traders' Camps—week-long classes for traders. Readers of this *Study Guide* are welcome to request a free subscription to his electronic newsletter by writing or calling:

Financial Trading, Inc.
P.O. Box 20555, Columbus Circle Station
New York, NY 10023, USA
Tel. 718-507-1033; fax 718-639-8889
e-mail: info@elder.com
website: www.elder.com